JAMS AND PRESERVES

more than 100 jam, chutney
and preserve recipes

CONTENTS

Making jams and preserves

How good it is to be able to eat fresh cherry jam on scones in mid-winter, or spicy, vegetable-laden chutneys with a barbecue in the height of summer. Preserving is a culinary technique that's both easy and satisfying to learn, and it rewards us with sweet and savoury produce to enjoy all year round.

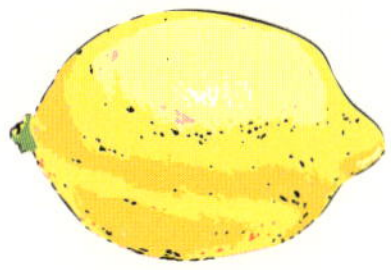

For centuries, jams, preserves, chutneys and pickles have been made to ensure a regular food supply during colder and leaner times. They are best made at the peak of the season when the fruit and vegetables are flavoursome, plentiful and inexpensive.

WHICH FRUIT TO CHOOSE

When making jams, preserves, chutneys or pickles, it is essential to use good-quality fruits and vegetables to obtain the best results. Always choose fruit that is firm and just ripe, and without any blemishes or bruises. Overripe fruit will lack the pectin needed to set the preserve. If the fruit is quite ripe, add about 10 per cent of underripe fruit to increase the pectin to the amount needed to set the preserve.

SUGAR and PECTIN

When making jams and jellies, the balance of the acid in the fruit, the sugar and the pectin will all play a part in the final firmness and flavour of the preserve. Sugar is not just used as a sweetener when making jams and jellies. It is also a preservative when used in a high concentration, inhibiting the development and growth of micro-organisms. To reach a high enough concentration, ¾–1 cup of sugar must be used per 1 cup of fruit. Sugar is also a setting agent and aids the setting process in jams and jellies which would not set without a commercial setting agent.

Pectin is found in the skin, flesh and seeds of most fruits in varying degrees. It is particularly high in citrus pith and apple skin. Some fruits are quite low in pectin or have none at all and need the addition of pectin-containing fruit or juice, or commercial setting agents, to help them set.

The acid level of the fruit is also important, because it acts as a preservative and setting agent. If low, acid levels can be supplemented with the addition of lemon juice or by combining several fruits in the one recipe. A commercial setting agent isn't always needed, and if the preserve sets when tested it may not be necessary to add it at all.

Successful jams and preserves require an even balance of pectin and acid. The chart below states the levels of pectin and acid found in fruits that are commonly used in jams and preserves.

TESTING FOR PECTIN

If you are not sure how much pectin is in the fruit you want to use for your jelly, place 2 teaspoons of methylated spirits in a small bowl and then gently add 1 teaspoon of the strained fruit mixture and stir gently. If there is enough pectin present to set the jelly, clots should form into one large lump. If they form smaller lumps, the mixture will need to be reduced some more or you will need to add some lemon juice. If the mixture is then still not setting, you may need to use a commercial setting agent. Follow the instructions on the packet.

SUGAR

You will notice that all our sweet preserve recipes call for warmed sugar. While warming the sugar before adding it to the pan is not absolutely imperative in a recipe and won't affect the final outcome, it does speed up the dissolving process. The sugar dissolves more quickly and, because it is warm, will not reduce the temperature of the fruit mixture as much as if you had added cold sugar. To warm sugar, spread it in an even layer in a deep-sided baking dish and warm in a slow oven 150°C (300°F/Gas 2) for 10–15 minutes, or until warmed through. Do not overheat the sugar or it will start to lump together. To make sure this

PECTIN AND ACID LEVELS IN FRUITS

HIGH PECTIN	MEDIUM PECTIN	LOW PECTIN	HIGH ACID	LOW ACID
blackcurrants	apricots	bananas	blackberries (early)	apricots
citrus fruits	blackberries (early)	blackberries (late)	blackcurrants	figs
cooking apples	eating apples	boysenberries	cherries	kiwi fruit
grapes	loganberries	cherries	citrus fruits	mangoes
plums (some varieties)	mulberries	figs	green apples	melons
quinces	peaches	guava	pineapple	passionfruit
redcurrants	pears	melons	plums	pears
	raspberries	nectarines	raspberries (early)	quinces
	rhubarb	passionfruit	redcurrants	rhubarb
	strawberries	pineapple		strawberries
				sweet apples

doesn't happen, stir the sugar once or twice while it is warming up. To save time, warm the sugar while you are cooking the fruit.

Do not add the sugar until the fruit has softened. If sugar is added before the fruit is fully soft, it will stay firm. Regular granulated sugar is used in our jam, jelly and preserve recipes unless otherwise specified. Caster (superfine) sugar is used in some recipes for quicker dissolving and better clarity. Brown sugar is used mostly in chutneys, pickles and relishes to enhance the flavours and give a deeper, rich colour.

EQUIPMENT

Good-quality, large, heavy-based stainless steel or enamel pans are one of the most important pieces of equipment you can have when making jams and preserves. And, if you are going to make large amounts on a regular basis, it's well worth buying special preserving pans.

Sugar thermometers are a very helpful gauge for temperatures. It is crucial, when bottling and sealing your preserve, that the temperature stays at or above 85°C (185°F). This will prevent the growth of potentially harmful bacteria. If you don't have a sugar thermometer, make sure you seal your preserve in its jar as soon as it is ready. You can also use your thermometer to test whether your preserve has reached setting point This generally occurs once the mixture has reached 104°C (220°F). However we haven't used this method much in this book, relying more on testing on a saucer with the wrinkle method.

Jam funnels make filling jars a little easier without the jam dripping down the sides. Large and small heatproof jugs are essential for pouring and measuring. A metal skimmer or metal spoon is ideal for removing scum from the surface of the jam or preserve. Ladles are often used to transfer cooked preserves to jars. Wooden spoons are needed for stirring, and, of course, a pastry brush to clean down the sides of the pan.

Muslin (cheesecloth) is used throughout this book both to drain liquids and to hold seeds and rind in a secure bundle. Muslin can be purchased at kitchenware or fabric stores. Alternatively, you can use a clean tea towel (dish towel). When you are straining mixtures such as jellies, ensure the

DEFINITIONS

JAM—made from small pieces of fruit and sugar, cooked to a thick, spreadable consistency.

PRESERVE—whole fruits preserved in a heavy, sugar-based syrup.

CONSERVE—whole or large pieces of fruit cooked with sugar until thick.

JELLY—made from the strained juice of cooked fruits, and sugar. Generally clear, but can contain small pieces of the original fruit.

MARMALADE—sliced, cooked citrus fruits, suspended in a sweet, thick jam mixture.

FRUIT PASTE—sieved, cooked fruit, cooked to a thick paste with sugar and cut into pieces when cold.

FRUIT CURD—thick, spreadable, creamy mixture made with juice, fruit purée and sometimes citrus rind, combined with sugar, eggs and butter and cooked until thick.

PICKLE—vegetables, or sometimes fruit, pickled in vinegar with sugar, salt and spices.

CHUTNEY—vegetables and/or fruit cooked with vinegar, sugar and spices to a thick consistency.

RELISH—salted cooked vegetables in a sugar, spice and vinegar-based sauce, which is thickened towards the end of cooking.

material is just damp so that it won't absorb too much of the liquid.

Before starting to cook your jam or preserve, ensure your equipment has been carefully washed in hot, soapy water and the jars you intend to use are thoroughly clean. Always make sure you have enough clean jars ready for when you have a pan full of boiling jam ready to bottle. The best way to ensure that jars are spotlessly clean is to preheat the oven to very slow 120°C (250°F/Gas ½). Thoroughly wash the jars and lids in hot, soapy water (or preferably in a dishwasher) and rinse well with hot water. Put the jars on baking trays and place them in the oven for 20 minutes, or until you are ready to use them. They must be dried fully in the oven.

HOW IT ALL WORKS

Whether you are making jams, preserves, jellies, pickles, chutneys or relishes, the method to use is essentially the same. Obviously, sweet jams, preserves and jellies require a lot more sugar than the savoury pickles, chutneys and relishes. They are also self-setting in that the mixture thickens on cooling to an easily spreadable consistency.

JAMS

Try not to cook too much jam all in one quantity. Do not use more than 2 kg (4 lb) fruit in a recipe at a time. You also need to make sure that your pan is large enough. Ideally, the mixture should be no more than 5–6 cm deep after the sugar has been added. Chutneys and pickles can be cooked in larger quantities, but remember that the more mixture you have in the pan, then the longer the cooking time. Jellies are generally cooked in smaller quantities.

Wash and dry the fruit well to remove any dirt. If you are using citrus fruits such as oranges or grapefruit, gently scrub the fruit with a soft bristle brush under warm running water to remove the wax coating. Remove any stalks from berries and cut away any damaged or bruised pieces of fruit (which you shouldn't have if you'd chosen your fruit carefully in the beginning). Cut up the fruit according to the recipe and place it into your pan to soften. Be aware that some recipes require the fruit to be soaked overnight. Reserved seeds and extra skin or fruit are used in many recipes in this book, particularly lemon pips and rind. These are wrapped in a square of muslin (cheesecloth) and can either be soaked overnight with the fruit, and then cooked with the fruit, as with marmalade, or simply added to the pan and cooked with the jam or preserve. For easy retrieval of the muslin bag, attach a long piece of string to the bag and tie it to the handle of the pan. The remaining ingredients are added according to each individual recipe.

The wrinkle test is a quick and easy way to see if jam has reached its setting point.

If the jam is not setting, cook a little longer and test again, using the second chilled plate.

If the jam is overcooked, it will be much thicker and darker than it should be.

> *"I value my garden more for being full of blackbirds than of cherries, and very frankly give them fruit for their songs.'*
>
> *Joseph Addison*
>
> *'The Spectator'. English essayist, poet & politician (1672–1719)*

Bring the mixture to the boil, then reduce the heat and simmer for the specified time until the fruit is tender. Then add the required amount of sugar. Remove any scum or foam from the top of the jam or preserve throughout the cooking process. The scum that forms on the top of the mixture is usually any impurities or dirt present on the fruit or sugar. Stir over the heat, without boiling, until all the sugar has dissolved. Brush the side of the pan with a pastry brush dipped in water, to dissolve any excess sugar crystals which can sometimes cause jams to crystallize towards the end of cooking. If the jam does crystallize, add 1–2 tablespoons of lemon juice and gently reheat. Be aware that this may change the taste slightly. Once all the sugar has dissolved, boil the mixture rapidly for the required time. Stir the jam often while it is cooking to speed up the cooking process and ensure that it does not stick to the bottom of the pan. After the specified cooking time is completed, or when the jam or preserve looks thick and syrupy, the mixture should fall from a wooden spoon heavily with 3 or 4 drops joining in a sheet as they drop. This means that the jam or preserve has reached its setting point.

Cooking times vary greatly between recipes, depending on pan sizes, the fruit used, the time of year, and if the fruit is in season, among other reasons. Therefore, it's necessary to test for setting point, sometimes up to 10 minutes before the stated time, to make sure the jam or preserve is ready to be bottled. Do not rely entirely on the times stated. Remove the pan from the heat, place 1 teaspoon of the jam on one of the cold plates and place it in the freezer for about 30 seconds, or until the jam has cooled to room temperature. Gently push through the jam with the tip of your finger. There should be a skin on top of the jam which should wrinkle. If it does wrinkle, it's ready. Ta da!! If not, then return the mixture briefly to the heat and try again in a few minutes with the second plate.

Immediately spoon or pour the mixture into the warm, clean jars. Pulpier jams tend to have a thicker consistency and jams with large pieces of fruit will need a few minutes standing in the pan

Any scum should be removed from the surface during cooking, using a skimmer.

Brush the side of the pan with a wet pastry brush to remove any sugar crystals.

Setting point has been reached when the jam drops from a spoon in thick sheets.

STICKY SITUATIONS

CRYSTALLIZATION—too much sugar was added to the fruit, and it was not dissolved properly before boiling.

TOUGH FRUIT—the fruit was not cooked long enough before the sugar was added. Fruit does not soften any further once sugar is added.

FRUIT FLOATS—the fruit was not cooked long enough or was not allowed to stand long enough before bottling.

TOO RUNNY—mixture has not set properly. Return it to the pan, bring to the boil again and retest for setting point before bottling.

MOULD—this can start to grow once the jar is opened, if storing in a warm place, or if the mixture was not covered while hot. If caught quickly, mould can be scooped off with a little jam and discarded. Refrigerate the remainder of the jam and eat as soon as possible.

FERMENTATION—mushy, overripe, bruised or damaged fruits were used in the cooking process, or insufficient sugar was added to the fruit mixture. If you do use less sugar in a recipe, make sure you eat the jam or preserve within a few months because it won't keep as long. The set won't be quite as firm. Keep in the refrigerator after opening

CLOUDINESS—this generally only occurs in jellies, when the jelly bag was squeezed or disturbed while the fruit was dripping through.

before bottling to allow the fruit to be evenly suspended in the mixture.

Don't leave the jam or jelly for too long or it will start to set in the pan. If this does happen, you will need to start all over again. Take care when pouring the preserves into the jars as the mixture is extremely hot. Hold the jar in a tea towel and pour or spoon in the preserve, filling right to the top. If your jars have small openings, it may be easier to first pour the jam into a clean heatproof jug then into the jars. You can also use a jam funnel.

Occasionally, you will find you have air bubbles in the bottles. To remove them, use a thin, clean skewer to help push the mixture to the side and release the bubble to the surface. This technique can be used for all types of preserves.

Alternatively, a gentle tap on a cloth on the bench will release some of the air bubbles. Seal the jars while the mixture is still hot. Turn jars upside down for 2 minutes, then invert them and leave to cool. This will ensure the fruit is evenly distributed and the lids are sterilized.

JELLIES

Choose fruits with a good pectin and acid balance for the best results. The fruit is cooked with or without water and then strained overnight in a damp jelly bag (available from good kitchenware stores) or a damp muslin bag suspended over a stool. A wide bowl is placed underneath to catch the liquid. Do not squeeze the jelly bag or the liquid and resulting jelly will turn cloudy. You can use the pectin test if necessary, but the recipes in this book give you the required amount of sugar for the fruit used. Add sugar, stir until dissolved and boil rapidly for the required time, following the same method for jams. Skimming off scum is essential at this stage or it will make the jelly cloudy later on. Before pouring into the clean, warm jars, be sure to allow any bubbles in the pan

to subside. Pour the jelly down the sides of the jars to prevent any bubbles forming.

SAVOURY PRESERVES

All the basics of jam making apply when cooking savoury preserves as well. Generally, they are cooked until thick and pulpy, not watery, and when tested on a plate will leave a clean trail behind without any runny liquid. Choose firm, ripe and unblemished vegetables. Always use clean, warm jars and equipment, and refrigerate the preserve after opening.

Savoury preserves contain a variety of herbs and spices. It is important to remember that dried herbs and spices do lose their flavour if kept too long and this can affect the final flavour of your preserve. It is best to buy in small, rather than large, quantities.

Testing for flavour while the preserve is hot doesn't always give a true indication of the final flavour. The flavours will only develop fully after a few weeks' storage. For a quick idea of the taste, allow a little to cool on a saucer before trying it. Ideally, before making changes to a recipe and adding new flavours, it is best to make the recipe first exactly as described in the book. Then, after storage, taste the preserve and work out what changes you'd like to make the next time you are cooking it.

CHUTNEYS

Long, slow cooking of both vegetables and fruit, with the addition of sugar, vinegar and spices so that the flavours and colours are both rich and concentrated, produces a thick, flavoursome pulp known as chutney. The flavour variations seem endless, depending on the fruit and vegetables used and the spices added.

Spices play a large part in chutney making and you can change a plain chutney into a deliciously spicy, aromatic one with the addition of chillies, cardamom and cinnamon, to name just a few. Just be careful not to add too many or you will overpower the flavours of the fruit in the chutney. Chutneys are cooked until very thick. They must be stirred often to prevent sticking and burning on the bottom of the pan. When tested on a plate, they should leave a clean trail behind without any runny liquid.

PICKLES

Preparing vegetables for pickling involves soaking them in a brine (salt and water solution) or layering them sprinkled with salt for 24 hours. The salt draws out moisture from the vegetables, which softens them and removes any excess liquid which may dilute the vinegar. It also adds to the final flavour. The vegetables should be rinsed well under cold running water after salting. They can

Use a clean, thin metal skewer to remove any air bubbles from the jars before sealing.

Curds are made of fruit, egg and butter and reach a thick, creamy consistency.

When tested, the chutney should leave a clean trail without any runny liquid.

STORAGE

JAMS, CONSERVES, PRESERVES—Store in an airtight jar in a cool, dark place for 6–12 months. Once opened, store in the refrigerator for 6 weeks.

JELLIES—Store in an airtight jar in a cool, dark place for 6–12 months. Once opened, store in refrigerator for 1 month.

CURDS—Store in an airtight jar in the refrigerator for up to 2 weeks.

FRUIT PASTES—Set in disposable foil trays or wrap in greaseproof paper, then plastic wrap, then foil and then plastic wrap again. Store in a cool, dark place for 6–12 months.

SAUCES, CHUTNEYS, RELISHES AND PICKLES—Sauces, chutneys, relishes and pickles should be left for 1 month before eating to allow the flavours to develop. Store in a cool, dark place for up to 1 year. Once opened, store refrigerated for 6 weeks.

HEAT-PROCESSED FRUITS AND VEGETABLES—Store in a cool, dark place for up to 1 year. Once opened, store in the refrigerator for 1 week.

MUSTARDS—Store in a cool, dark place for up to 3 months. Once jars are opened, refrigerate only for 1–2 weeks.

be left raw or lightly cooked and are packed into clean jars and topped with a vinegar solution. Spices can also be added to increase the flavour.

RELISHES

The method for making relishes is very similar to that for making pickles. First salt the vegetables, then rinse them well under cold, running water. The vegetable mixture is then simmered in a spicy vinegar solution before being thickened with cornflour (cornstarch) or a slurry—a thin paste made from plain (all-purpose) flour and water.

CURDS

Gently cooked over a pan of simmering water, curds still require that the basics of jam making are followed. The egg and butter thicken the fruit mixture during cooking and once refrigerated.

FRUIT PASTES

Fruit pastes are a cross between jelly and jam. It is a sieved fruit purée, cooked with sugar until thick and paste like. Again, the basics of jam making apply here, and great care is needed to avoid being splattered with the thick mixture as it bubbles like hot lava in the base of the pan. Take care not to overcook the mixture or let it catch and burn on the bottom. Fruit pastes use a large amount of fruit, so it is best to make them when there is an overabundance available at a reasonable price.

Lemon pips and rind are often added to the cooking mixture in a small muslin (cheesecloth) bag.

SWEET JAMS AND PRESERVES

Strawberry jam

INGREDIENTS
1.5 kg (3 lb/about 10 cups) strawberries
125 ml (4 fl oz/½ cup) lemon juice
1.25 kg (2 lb 8 oz/5½ cups) sugar, warmed

Put two small plates in the freezer for testing purposes (you may not need the second plate). Wipe the strawberries clean, then hull them and place in a large pan with lemon juice, warmed sugar and 125 ml (4 fl oz/½ cup) water. Warm gently, without boiling, stirring gently with a wooden spoon, trying not to break up the berries too much.

Increase the heat and, without boiling, stir the mixture for 10 minutes, or until all the sugar has dissolved. Increase the heat and boil for 20 minutes, stirring often. Skim any scum off the surface with a skimmer or slotted spoon. Start testing for setting point after 20 minutes, but it may take up to 40 minutes for the jam to be ready. Be careful that the jam does not catch on the base of the pan and start to burn.

Remove from the heat, place a little jam on one of the cold plates and place in the freezer for 30 seconds. When setting point is reached, a skin will form on the surface and the jam will wrinkle when pushed with your finger. Remove any scum from the surface.

Spoon immediately into clean, warm jars and seal. Turn the jars upside down for 2 minutes, then invert and leave to cool. Label and date. Store in a cool, dark place for 6–12 months. Refrigerate after opening for up to 6 weeks.

note DO NOT WASH STRAWBERRIES ONCE THEY HAVE BEEN HULLED. AS THEY WILL ABSORB WATER AND THEIR TASTE AND TEXTURE WILL BE AFFECTED.

preparation 15 minutes * cooking 1 hour

Swiss roll *with strawberry jam*

Here is a cake that looks impressive but is easy to prepare. Just be sure to roll up the sponge slowly and carefully. For a treat, spread a layer of whipped cream over the jam.

INGREDIENTS

90 g (3¼ oz/¾ cup) self-raising flour
3 eggs, lightly beaten
170 g (6 oz/¾ cup) caster (superfine) sugar
160 g (6 oz/½ cup) strawberry jam (recipe on previous page), beaten
icing (confectioners') sugar, to sprinkle

Preheat the oven to 190°C (375°F/Gas 5). Lightly grease a shallow 2 x 25 x 30 cm (¾ x 10 x 12 inch) Swiss roll tin (jelly roll tin) and line the base with baking paper, extending over the two long sides. Sift the flour three times onto baking paper.

Beat the eggs using electric beaters in a small bowl for 5 minutes, or until thick and pale. Add 115 g (4 oz/½ cup) of the sugar gradually, beating constantly until the mixture is pale and glossy. Transfer to a large bowl. Using a metal spoon, fold in the flour quickly and lightly. Spread into the tin and smooth the surface. Bake for 10–12 minutes, or until lightly golden and springy to touch. Meanwhile, place a clean tea towel (dish towel) on a work surface, cover with baking paper and lightly sprinkle with the remaining caster sugar. When the cake is cooked, turn it out immediately onto the sugar.

Using the tea towel as a guide, carefully roll the cake up from the short side, rolling the paper inside the roll. Stand the rolled cake on a wire rack for 5 minutes, then carefully unroll and allow the cake to cool to room temperature. Spread with the jam and re-roll. Trim the ends with a knife. Sprinkle with icing sugar.

preparation 25 minutes ✦ cooking 12 minutes ✦ serves 10

Fig preserve

INGREDIENTS

1 kg (2 lb 4 oz) fresh figs, stalks removed
125 ml (4 fl oz/½ cup) lemon juice
1 kg (2 lb 4 oz/4⅓ cups) sugar, warmed

Put two small plates in the freezer for testing purposes (you may not need the second plate). Put the figs in a large heatproof bowl. Cover with boiling water for 3 minutes. Drain, cool and cut into pieces.

Place the figs, lemon juice and 125 ml (4 fl oz/½ cup) water in a large pan. Bring to the boil, then reduce the heat and simmer, covered, for 20 minutes, or until the figs are soft. Add the sugar and stir over medium heat, without boiling, for 5 minutes, or until all the sugar has dissolved.

Bring to the boil and boil for 20 minutes, stirring often. Remove any scum from the surface during cooking with a skimmer or a slotted spoon. Add a little water if the mixture thickens too much. When it is thick and pulpy, start testing for setting point.

Remove from the heat, place a little preserve on one cold of the cold plates and place in the freezer for 30 seconds. When setting point is reached, a skin will form on the surface and the preserve will wrinkle when pushed with your finger. Remove any scum from the surface.

Pour immediately into clean, warm jars, and seal. Turn the jars upside down for 2 minutes, then invert and leave to cool. Label and date. Store in a cool, dark place for 6–12 months. Refrigerate preserve after opening for up to 6 weeks.

preparation 20 minutes ✦ cooking 45 minutes

Fig and raspberry cake *with fig preserve*

This shortcake is best eaten on the day it is made. The slightly earthy taste of the figs and the intense flavour of fresh raspberries and citrus meld beautifully in this dessert.

INGREDIENTS

185 g (6½ oz) unsalted butter
185 g (6½ oz/¾ cup) caster (superfine) sugar
1 egg
1 egg yolk
335 g (11¾ oz/2⅔ cups) plain (all-purpose) flour
1 teaspoon baking powder
4 figs, quartered
grated zest of 1 orange
200 g (7 oz/1⅔ cups) raspberries
2 tablespoons sugar, extra
fig preserve (recipe on previous page)
whipped cream or mascarpone cheese, to serve

Preheat the oven to 180°C (450°F/Gas 4). Grease a 23 cm (9 inch) spring-form cake tin.

Cream the butter and sugar in a bowl until light and pale. Add the egg and egg yolk and beat again. Sift the flour and baking powder into the bowl and add a pinch of salt. Stir to combine. Chill for 15 minutes, or until firm enough to roll out.

Divide the dough in two equal halves and roll out one half large enough to fit the base of the tin. Cover with the figs, orange zest and raspberries. Roll out the remaining dough and place it over the filling. Lightly brush the top with water and sprinkle with the extra sugar. Bake for 30 minutes, or until a skewer inserted into the centre of the cake comes out clean. Cut into slices. Stir a little fig preserve gently through whipped cream or mascarpone cheese and serve on the side.

preparation 25 minutes ✦ cooking 30 minutes

THE FRUIT OF LEGEND

One of the most sensual of fruits, with their velvety skins and seed-filled flesh, figs held mythological status in ancient Rome and Greece where they were not only a chief source of sustenance for the original Olympians, but so important to the Greek diet that it became illegal to export them.

Mixed berry jam

INGREDIENTS

1 kg (2 lb 4 oz/about 7 cups) mixed berries (strawberries, raspberries, blackberries, blueberries, mulberries)
80 ml (2½ fl oz/⅓ cup) lemon juice
1 kg (2 lb 4 oz/4⅓ cups) sugar, warmed
25 g (¾ oz) jam setting mixture

Place the berries and lemon juice in a large pan and gently cook for 10 minutes. Add the sugar and stir over low heat for 5 minutes, or until all the sugar has dissolved.

Boil for 15 minutes, stirring often, and then remove from the heat. Add the jam setting mixture, then return the berry mixture to the heat and boil rapidly for a further 5 minutes. Remove any scum from the surface with a skimmer or slotted spoon.

Pour immediately into clean, warm jars, and seal. Turn the jars upside down for 2 minutes, then invert and leave to cool. Label and date. Store the jars in a cool, dark place for 6–12 months. Refrigerate after opening for up to 6 weeks.

note Remove the stems, stalks, leaves and any blemishes from the berries you have chosen. If the berries are sandy or gritty, wash them gently under cold water and drain well in a colander to remove as much water as possible before use. Use a mixture of fresh and frozen berries, if necessary.

preparation 20 minutes ✦ cooking 35 minutes

SCONES

310 g (11 oz/2½ cups) self-raising flour
1 teaspoon baking powder
40 g (1½ oz) chilled unsalted butter cut into small cubes
250 ml (9 fl oz/1 cup) milk (or half buttermilk, half milk)

Preheat oven to 220°C (425°F/Gas 7). Lightly grease a baking tray or line with baking paper. Sift the flour, baking powder and a pinch of salt into a bowl. Using your fingertips, rub in the butter briefly and lightly until mixture resembles fine breadcrumbs. Mix in the sugar. Make a well in the centre. Pour in almost all of the milk and mix with a flat-bladed knife, using a cutting action until dough comes together in clumps. Rotate the bowl as you work. Use the remaining milk if the mixture seems dry. Handle mixture with great care and a very light hand. Dough should feel slightly wet and sticky. With floured hands, gently gather the dough together, lift onto a lightly floured surface and pat into a smooth ball. Do not knead or the scones will be tough.

Pat or lightly roll the dough out to 2 cm (¾ inch) thick. Using a floured 6 cm (2½ inch) cutter, cut into rounds. Don't pat out too thinly or the scones will not be a good height. Gather scraps together and, without over-handling them, press out as before and cut out more rounds. Place close together on the baking tray and lightly brush the tops with milk.

Bake in the top half of the oven for 12–15 minutes, or until risen and golden. If you aren't sure if they are cooked, break one open. If still doughy in the centre, cook for a few more minutes. For soft scones, wrap in a dry tea towel (dish towel) while hot. For scones with a crisp top, transfer to a wire rack to cool slightly before wrapping. Serve warm with a jam and cream.

Preparation 20 minutes
Cooking 12–15 minutes
Makes 10–12 scones.

Apricot and passionfruit jam

INGREDIENTS

1.2 kg (2 lb 6 oz) fresh apricots, stones removed

1 kg (2 lb 4 oz/4⅓ cups) sugar, warmed

160 g (5½ oz/⅔ cup) passionfruit pulp

2 tablespoons lemon juice

Put two small plates in the freezer for testing purposes (you may not need the second plate). Cut apricots into quarters and place in a large pan with 80 ml (2½ fl oz/⅓ cup) water. Cover and cook over low heat for 10 minutes, or until tender.

Remove from the heat and add the sugar, passionfruit pulp and lemon juice. Heat slowly, stirring, for about 5 minutes, or until all the sugar has dissolved. Return to the boil and boil rapidly for 30 minutes, stirring often. Remove any scum during cooking with a skimmer or slotted spoon. When the jam falls from a tilted wooden spoon in thick sheets without dripping, start testing for setting point.

Remove from the heat, place a little jam on one of the cold plates and place in the freezer for 30 seconds. When setting point is reached, a skin will form on the surface and the jam will wrinkle when pushed with your finger. Remove any scum from the surface.

Spoon immediately into clean, warm jars and seal. Turn the jars upside down for 2 minutes, then invert and leave to cool. Label and date. Store in a cool, dark place for 6–12 months. Refrigerate after opening for up to 6 weeks.

preparation 15 minutes * cooking 45 minutes

Raspberry jam

INGREDIENTS

1.5 kg (3 lb/about 12 cups) fresh or frozen raspberries
80 ml (2½ fl oz/⅓ cup) lemon juice
1.5 kg (3 lb/6½ cups) sugar, warmed

Put two small plates in the freezer for testing purposes (you may not need the second plate). Place the berries and lemon juice in a large pan. Stir over low heat for 10 minutes, or until the berries are soft.

Add the sugar and stir, without boiling, for 5 minutes, or until all the sugar has dissolved.

Bring the mixture to the boil and boil for 20 minutes. Stir often and make sure the jam doesn't stick or burn on the base of the pan. Remove any scum during cooking with a skimmer or slotted spoon. When the jam falls from a tilted wooden spoon in thick sheets without dripping, start testing for setting point.

Remove from the heat, place a little jam on one of the cold plates and place in the freezer for 30 seconds. When setting point is reached, a skin will form on the surface and the jam will wrinkle when pushed with your finger. Remove any scum.

Spoon immediately into clean, warm jars and seal. Turn the jars upside down for 2 minutes, then invert and leave to cool. Label and date. Store in a cool, dark place for 6–12 months. Refrigerate after opening for up to 6 weeks.

note FROZEN RASPBERRIES CAN BE USED, BUT THE COOKING TIME SHOULD BE INCREASED BY A FEW MINUTES.

preparation 10 minutes * cooking 35 minutes

Princess fingers *with raspberry jam*

Slices are the perfect thing to make for a morning or afternoon tea party. This attractive one is packed with nuts, jam and coconut and can be made a couple of days in advance.

INGREDIENTS

125 g (4½ oz) unsalted butter, cubed and softened
80 g (2¾ oz/⅓ cup) caster (superfine) sugar
1 teaspoon natural vanilla extract
2 egg yolks
250 g (9 oz/2 cups) plain (all-purpose) flour
1 teaspoon baking powder
1 tablespoon milk
160 g (5¾ oz/½ cup) raspberry jam (recipe on previous page
40 g (1½ oz/⅓ cup) chopped walnuts
80 g (2¾ oz/⅓ cup) chopped red glacé cherries
2 egg whites
1 tablespoon grated orange zest
115 g (4 oz/½ cup) caster (superfine) sugar, extra
45 g (1¾ oz/½ cup) desiccated coconut
30 g (1 oz/1 cup) puffed rice cereal

Preheat the oven to 180°C (350°F/Gas 4). Lightly grease a 20 x 30 cm (8 x 12 inch) shallow tin and line with baking paper, leaving the paper hanging over on the two long sides. Cream the butter, sugar and vanilla using electric beaters until light and fluffy. Add the egg yolks, one at a time, beating well after each addition.

Sift flour and baking powder into a bowl, then fold into the creamed mixture with a metal spoon. Fold in the milk, then press evenly and firmly into the tin. Spread the jam over the surface and sprinkle with the chopped walnuts and cherries.

Beat the egg whites in a small, dry bowl until stiff peaks form. Fold in the orange zest and extra sugar with a metal spoon, then fold in the coconut and puffed rice cereal. Spread over the slice with a metal spatula.

Bake for 30–35 minutes, or until firm and golden brown. Cool the slice in the tin. Lift out the slice, using the paper as handles, and cut into fingers. This slice can be kept for up to 4 days in an airtight container.

preparation 35 minutes ✦ cooking 35 minutes ✦ makes 24 pieces

Blueberry preserve

INGREDIENTS

1 kg (2 lb 4 oz/about 6 cups) blueberries
60 ml (2 fl oz/¼ cup) lemon juice (and the pips of 1 lemon)
1 kg (2 lb 4 oz/4⅓ cups) sugar, warmed

Put two small plates in the freezer for testing purposes (you may not need the second plate). Place berries in a large pan with 185 ml (6 fl oz/¾ cup) water. Place the lemon pips on a piece of muslin (cheesecloth) and tie securely with string. Add to the pan. Cook over low heat for 5 minutes, or until the berries just start to colour the water.

Add the lemon juice and sugar, and stir over low heat for 5 minutes, or until all the sugar has dissolved. Bring slowly to the boil and cook for 20–25 minutes, stirring often. Remove any scum during cooking with a skimmer or slotted spoon. When the preserve falls from a tilted wooden spoon in thick sheets without dripping, start testing for setting point.

Remove from the heat, place a little preserve on one of the cold plates. Place in the freezer for 30 seconds. When setting point is reached, a skin will form on the surface and the preserve will wrinkle when pushed with your finger. Remove any scum from the surface.

Transfer to a heatproof jug and pour immediately into clean, warm jars and seal. Turn the jars upside down for 2 minutes, then invert and leave to cool. Label and date. Store in a cool, dark place for 6–12 months. Refrigerate after opening for up to 6 weeks.

preparation 10 minutes * cooking 35 minutes

Peach conserve

INGREDIENTS

1.5 kg (3 lb 5 oz) peaches (about 9 large peaches)
1 green apple
1 lemon
1 kg (2 lb 4 oz/4⅓ cups) sugar, warmed

Put two small plates in the freezer for testing purposes (you may not need the second plate). Score a cross in the base of each peach. Place peaches in a large heatproof bowl and cover with boiling water. Leave for 1–2 minutes, then remove with a slotted spoon. Cool slightly and peel. Halve, remove the stone and chop flesh into 2 cm (1 inch) pieces.

Chop the apple, including the peel and core, into 1 cm (½ inch) pieces. Peel thin strips of rind from the lemon, then cut it in half and juice. Place the apple and lemon rind onto a square of muslin (cheesecloth) and tie securely with string.

Place the chopped peaches, muslin bag and 310 ml (11 fl oz/1¼ cups) water in a large pan. Bring slowly to the boil, then reduce the heat and simmer for 30 minutes, or until the peaches are tender. Remove any scum from the surface during cooking with a skimmer or slotted spoon. Squeeze any excess juice from the muslin bag by pushing firmly against the side of the pan, then discard the bag.

Add the sugar and stir over low heat for 5 minutes, or until all the sugar has dissolved. Add the lemon juice, return to the boil and boil rapidly for 30 minutes, stirring often. Stir across the base of the pan to check that the conserve is not sticking or burning. When the conserve falls from a tilted wooden spoon in thick sheets without dripping, start testing for setting point.

Remove from heat, place a little conserve on one of the cold plates and place in the freezer for 30 seconds. When setting point is reached, a skin will form on the surface and the conserve will wrinkle when pushed with your finger. Remove any scum from the surface.

Spoon immediately into clean, warm jars and seal. Turn the jars upside down for 2 minutes, then invert and leave to cool. Label and date. Store in a cool, dark place for 6–12 months. Refrigerate after opening for up to 6 weeks.

preparation 20 minutes ✦ cooking 1 hour 5 minutes

Tomato and pineapple jam

INGREDIENTS

2 kg (4 lb 8 oz) ripe tomatoes
1.5 kg (3 lb 5 oz/6½ cups) sugar, warmed
125 ml (4 fl oz/½ cup) lemon juice
440 g (14 oz/2¾ cups) can crushed pineapple, drained

Put two small plates in the freezer for testing purposes (you may not need the second plate). Cut a cross in the base of each tomato. Place tomatoes in a large bowl, cover with boiling water and leave for 30 seconds, or until the skins start to spilt. Transfer tomatoes to a bowl of cold water. Remove skin and chop the flesh.

Place the tomato in a large pan. Add half the warmed sugar and simmer for 5–10 minutes over low heat, stirring, until the tomato has softened and all the sugar has dissolved.

Add the lemon juice, pineapple and remaining sugar. Stir over low heat until all the sugar has dissolved. Bring to the boil and cook for 30–35 minutes, stirring frequently. Remove any scum from the surface during cooking with a skimmer or slotted spoon. When the jam falls from a tilted wooden spoon in thick sheets without dripping, start testing for setting point.

Remove from the heat, place a little jam on one of the cold plates and place in the freezer for 30 seconds. When setting point is reached, a skin will form on the surface and the jam will wrinkle when pushed with your finger. Remove any scum from the surface.

Spoon immediately into clean, warm jars and seal. Turn the jars upside down for 2 minutes, then invert and leave to cool. Label and date. Store in a cool, dark place for 6–12 months. Refrigerate after opening for up to 6 weeks.

note CHOOSE TOMATOES THAT ARE VERY RIPE TO MAXIMISE THE TASTE OF YOUR JAM. VINE-RIPENED TOMATOES, WHILE EXPENSIVE, GENERALLY HAVE THE BEST FLAVOUR.

preparation 20 minutes * cooking 35 minutes

Blood plum jam

INGREDIENTS
2 kg (4 lb 8 oz) blood plums
125 ml (4 fl oz/½ cup) lemon juice
1.5 kg (3 lb 5 oz/6½ cups) sugar, warmed

Put two small plates in the freezer for testing purposes (you may not need the second plate). Cut plums in half and remove the stones. Crack a few stones and remove the kernels. Place the kernels in a piece of muslin (cheesecloth) and tie securely with string. Place the plums and the bag in a large pan and add 1 litre (4 cups) water. Bring slowly to the boil, reduce the heat and simmer, covered, for 50 minutes, or until the fruit has softened.

Add the lemon juice and sugar and stir over low heat, without boiling, for 5 minutes, or until all the sugar has dissolved. Bring to the boil and boil for 20 minutes, stirring often. Remove any scum from the surface during cooking with a skimmer or slotted spoon. When the jam falls from a tilted wooden spoon in thick sheets without dripping, start testing for setting point.

Remove from the heat, place a little jam on one of the cold plates and place in the freezer for 30 seconds. When setting point is reached, a skin will form on the surface and the jam will wrinkle when pushed with your finger. Remove any scum from the surface.

Spoon immediately into clean, warm jars and seal. Turn the jars upside down for 2 minutes, then invert and leave to cool. Label and date. Store in a cool, dark place for 6–12 months. Refrigerate after opening for up to 6 weeks.

note Blood plums have dark skin and dark flesh. If unavailable, any kind of plum can be used.

preparation 20 minutes * cooking 1 hour 15 minutes

A STICKY BUSINESS

Plums don't contain much pectin, which helps jam set. To avoid the problem, crack a few of the plum stones and remove the kernels. Tie them in a little muslin bag and add to the cooking jam to assist in setting.

Monte creams *with blood plum jam*

It is said that this childhood (and adult) favourite takes its name from the glamorous city of Monte Carlo. Whatever the reason, it's a delicious cookie.

INGREDIENTS

125 g (4½ oz) unsalted butter
115 g (4 oz/½ cup) caster (superfine) sugar
60 ml (2 fl oz/¼ cup) milk
185 g (6½ oz/1½ cups) self-raising flour
30 g (1 oz/¼ cup) custard powder or instant vanilla pudding mix
30 g (1 oz/⅓ cup) desiccated coconut
custard powder or instant vanilla pudding mix, extra

FILLING

75 g (2¾ oz) unsalted butter, softened
85 g (3 oz/⅔ cup) icing (confectioners') sugar
2 teaspoons milk
105 g (3¾ oz/⅓ cup) blood plum jam (recipe on page 39)

Preheat the oven to 180°C (350°F/Gas 4). Line two baking trays with baking paper. Cream the butter and sugar in a small bowl using electric beaters until light and fluffy. Add the milk and beat until combined. Sift the flour and custard powder and add to the bowl with the coconut. Mix to form a soft dough.

Roll 2 teaspoons of the mixture into balls. Place on the trays and press with a fork. Dip the fork in the extra custard powder occasionally to prevent it from sticking. Bake for 15–20 minutes, or until just golden. Transfer to a wire rack to cool completely before filling.

To make the filling, beat the butter and icing sugar in a small bowl using electric beaters until light and creamy. Beat in the milk. Spread one biscuit with ½ teaspoon of the filling and one with ½ teaspoon of jam, then press them together.

preparation 30 minutes ✦ cooking 20 minutes ✦ makes 25

Rhubarb and ginger jam

INGREDIENTS

1.5 kg (3 lb 5 oz) trimmed rhubarb (leaves and ends removed)
1.5 kg (3 lb 5 oz) sugar, warmed
125 ml (4 fl oz/½ cup) lemon juice
4 cm (1½ inch) piece fresh ginger, bruised and halved
100 g (3½ oz) glacé (candied) ginger

Chop the rhubarb into small pieces. Layer the rhubarb, sugar and lemon juice in a large non-metallic bowl. Cover and leave overnight.

Put two small plates in the freezer for testing purposes (you may not need the second plate). Place the rhubarb mixture in a large pan. Finely chop the fresh ginger and place on a square of muslin (cheesecloth). Tie securely with string and add to the pan. Stir over a low heat for 5 minutes, or until all the sugar has dissolved. Bring to the boil and boil rapidly for 20–30 minutes, stirring often. Remove any scum during cooking with a skimmer or slotted spoon. When the jam falls from a tilted wooden spoon in thick sheets without dripping, start testing for setting point.

Remove from the heat, place a little jam on one of the cold plates and place in the freezer for 30 seconds. When setting point is reached, a skin will form on the surface and the jam will wrinkle when pushed with your finger. Remove any scum and discard the muslin bag. Finely chop the glacé ginger and add to the pan.

Spoon immediately into clean, warm jars, and seal. Turn jars upside down for 2 minutes, then invert and leave to cool. Label and date. Store in a cool, dark place for 6–12 months. Refrigerate after opening for up to 6 weeks.

note THE AMOUNT OF GINGER CAN BE VARIED, ACCORDING TO TASTE.

preparation 15 minutes + overnight soaking ✦ cooking 35 minutes

Apricot jam

INGREDIENTS

1 kg (2 lb 4 oz) apricots, stones removed, quartered

1 kg (2 lb 4 oz/4⅓ cups) sugar, warmed

Put two small plates in the freezer for testing purposes (you may not need the second plate).

Put the apricots in a large pan with 375 ml (13 fl oz/1½ cups) water. Bring to the boil, stirring, for 20 minutes, or until the fruit has softened.

Add the sugar and stir, without boiling, for 5 minutes, or until all the sugar has dissolved. Return to the boil and boil for 20 minutes, stirring often. Stir across the base of the pan to check that the jam is not sticking or burning. Remove any scum during cooking with a skimmer or slotted spoon. When the jam falls from a tilted wooden spoon in thick sheets without dripping, start testing for setting point.

Remove from the heat, place a little jam on one of the cold plates and place in the freezer for 30 seconds. When setting point is reached, a skin will form on the surface and the jam will wrinkle when pushed with your finger. Remove any scum.

Spoon immediately into clean, warm jars and seal. Turn the jars upside down for 2 minutes, then invert and leave to cool. Label and date. Store in a cool, dark place for 6–12 months. Refrigerate after opening for up to 6 weeks.

preparation 20 minutes * cooking 45 minutes

Frozen berry jam

INGREDIENTS

300 g (10 oz/2¼ cups) frozen blackberries
300 g (10 oz/2¼ cups) frozen raspberries
300 g (10 oz/2¼ cups) frozen blueberries
60 ml (2 fl oz/¼ cup) lemon juice, reserving any pips
750 g (1 lb 10 oz/3 cups) sugar, warmed

Put two small plates in the freezer for testing purposes (you may not need the second plate). Put frozen berries in a large pan with 750 ml (26 fl oz/3 cups) water and the lemon juice.

Place the pips on a square of muslin (cheesecloth) and tie securely with string. Add to the pan. Bring to the boil, then reduce the heat and simmer for 30 minutes.

Add the sugar and stir over low heat for 5 minutes, or until all the sugar has dissolved. Return to the boil and boil for 30–40 minutes, stirring often. Remove any scum during cooking with a skimmer or slotted spoon. When the jam falls from a tilted wooden spoon in thick sheets without dripping, start testing for setting point.

Remove from the heat, place a little jam on one of the cold plates and place in the freezer for 30 seconds. A skin will form on the surface and the jam will wrinkle when pushed with your finger when setting point is reached. Discard the muslin bag. Remove any scum from the surface.

Spoon immediately into clean, warm jars and seal. Turn the jars upside down for 2 minutes, then invert and leave to cool. Label and date. Store in a cool, dark place for 6–12 months. Refrigerate after opening for up to 6 weeks.

preparation 10 minutes ✦ cooking 1 hour 15 minutes

Banana jam

INGREDIENTS

1 kg (2 lb 4 oz) very ripe bananas (about 7), peeled (see Note)
100 ml (3½ fl oz) lemon juice
750 g (1 lb 10 oz/3 cups) sugar, warmed

Chop the bananas and place in a large pan with the lemon juice and sugar. Bring to the boil and skim any scum with a skimmer or slotted spoon.

Cook the jam over medium heat for 30 minutes, then reduce the heat and simmer, stirring frequently, for 15–20 minutes, or until the jam is thick and pale red in colour. Remove any scum from the surface.

Spoon immediately into clean, warm jars, and seal. Turn jars upside down for 2 minutes, then invert and leave to cool. Label and date. Store in a cool, dark place for 6–12 months. Refrigerate after opening for up to 6 weeks.

notes Use very mushy bananas, similar to those you would use for a banana cake. While not a true jam, this is just as delicious. Serve as you would other fruit jams.

preparation 10 minutes ✦ cooking 50 minutes

Banana muffins *with banana jam*

Every lunchbox deserves a good muffin, and this recipe delivers. Moist and light, they are even better at teatime spread with a generous amount of banana jam.

INGREDIENTS

310 g (11 oz/2½ cups) self-raising flour
170 g (6 oz/¾ cup) caster (superfine) sugar
½ teaspoon ground mixed (pumpkin pie) spice
250 ml (9 fl oz/1 cup) milk
2 eggs, lightly beaten
1 teaspoon natural vanilla extract
150 g (5½ oz) unsalted butter, melted and cooled
240 g (9 oz/1 cup) mashed ripe banana
banana jam, for spreading (recipe on previous page)

Preheat the oven to 200°C (400°F/Gas 6). Lightly grease a 12-hole standard muffin tin, or line the muffin tin with paper cases. Sift the flour into a bowl. Add the sugar and mixed spice to the bowl and stir through the flour. Make a well in the centre.

Mix together the milk, egg and vanilla. Pour the liquid into the well in the flour and add the cooled butter and banana. Fold the mixture gently with a metal spoon until just combined. Do not overmix — the batter will still be slightly lumpy. Divide the mixture evenly among the holes — fill each hole to about three-quarters full.

Bake the muffins for 20–25 minutes, or until they are golden and a skewer inserted into the centre of a muffin comes out clean. Leave the muffins in the tin for a couple of minutes to cool. Gently loosen each muffin with a flat-bladed knife before turning out onto a wire rack. Serve warm or at room temperature, spread with banana jam.

preparation 20 minutes ✦ cooking 25 minutes ✦ makes 12

Traditional fruit mince

INGREDIENTS

2 large green apples (about 440 g/14 oz), peeled, cored and finely chopped
250 g (8 oz) packet suet mix
345 g (12 oz/1½ cups), firmly packed soft brown sugar
375 g (12 oz/3 cups) raisins
250 g (8 oz/2 cups) sultanas
250 g (8 oz/2 cups) currants
150 g (5 oz/¾ cup) mixed peel
100 g (3½ oz) slivered almonds, chopped
1 tablespoon mixed spice
½ teaspoon nutmeg
½ teaspoon cinnamon
2 teaspoons grated orange rind
1 teaspoon grated lemon rind
250 ml (9 fl oz/1 cup) orange juice
125 ml (8 fl oz/½ cup) lemon juice
150 ml (5 fl oz) brandy

Combine all the ingredients and 125 ml (4 fl oz/½ cup) of the brandy in a large bowl. Combine thoroughly.

Spoon the fruit mince into clean, warm jars. Use a skewer to remove air bubbles and to pack the mixture in firmly. Leave a 1.5 cm (½ inch) space at the top of the jar and wipe the jar clean with a cloth. Spoon remaining brandy over the surface of the fruit mince and seal. Label and date.

Set aside for at least 3 weeks, or up to 6 months, before using in pies and tarts. Keep the fruit mince refrigerated in hot weather.

preparation 20 minutes ✦ no cooking required

FRUIT MINCE SLICE

250 g (9 oz/2 cups) plain (all-purpose) flour
60 g (2¼ oz/½ cup) icing (confectioners') sugar
185 g (6½ oz) unsalted butter, cubed
1 egg
410 g (14½ oz) fruit mince (mincemeat)
150 g (5½ oz) pitted prunes, chopped
100 g (3½ oz) glacé ginger, chopped
1 egg, lightly beaten
icing (confectioners') sugar, extra, to dust

Preheat the oven to 190°C (375°F/Gas 5). Lightly grease a shallow 18 x 28 cm (7 x 11¼ inch) tin and line base with baking paper, leaving the paper hanging over the two long sides. Sift the flour and icing sugar into a large bowl. Rub in the butter with your fingertips until the mixture resembles fine breadcrumbs. Make a well in the centre and add the egg. Mix with a flat-bladed knife, using a cutting action, until the mixture comes together. Turn onto a lightly floured surface and press together until smooth.

Divide the dough in half and press one portion into the tin. Bake for 10 minutes, then leave to cool. Roll remaining pastry out on a piece of baking paper; refrigerate for 15 minutes. Spread the fruit mince evenly over the baked pastry, topping it with the prunes and ginger. Cut the rolled pastry into thin strips with a sharp knife or fluted pastry wheel. Arrange on top of the fruit in a diagonal lattice pattern. Brush with the beaten egg. Bake for 30 minutes, or until golden. Cool in the tin, then lift out, using the paper as handles, and cut into squares or fingers. Serve dusted with icing sugar. The slice can be kept for up to 4 days if stored in an airtight container in a cool place, or in the refrigerator.

PREPARATION 20 MINUTES
COOKING 40 MINUTES
MAKES 15

Fruit mince pies *using traditional fruit mince*

A warm mince pie on a cold winter's day is a very comforting thing. And, mince pies are, of course, synonymous with Christmas fare.

INGREDIENTS

PASTRY

250 g (9 oz/2 cups) plain (all-purpose) flour

150 g (5½ oz) chilled unsalted butter, cubed

85 g (3 oz/⅔ cup) icing (confectioners') sugar

2–3 tablespoons iced water

icing (confectioners') sugar, extra, to dust

traditional fruit mince (recipe on previous page)

Preheat the oven to 180°C (350°F/Gas 4). Lightly grease two 12-hole shallow patty pans or mini muffin tins.

To make the pastry, sift the flour into a bowl. Using your fingertips, rub in the butter until the mixture resembles fine breadcrumbs. Stir in the icing sugar and make a well in the centre. Add almost all the water and mix with a flat-bladed knife, using a cutting action, until the mixture comes together in beads. Add the remaining water if the dough is too dry. Turn out onto a lightly floured work surface and gather into a ball. Roll out two-thirds of the pastry and cut out 24 rounds, slightly larger than the holes in the patty pans, with a round fluted cutter. Fit the rounds into the tins.

Divide the fruit mince evenly among the pastry cases. Roll out the remaining pastry, a little thinner than before, and cut 12 rounds with the same cutter. Using a smaller fluted cutter, cut 12 more rounds. Place the large circles on top of half the pies and press the edges to seal. Place the smaller circles on the remainder. Bake for 25 minutes, or until golden. Leave in the tins for 5 minutes, then lift out with a knife and cool on wire racks. Dust lightly with icing sugar. Eat within a couple of days.

preparation 30 minutes ✦ cooking 25 minutes ✦ makes 24

Pineapple and mango jam

INGREDIENTS

1 ripe pineapple

2 large mangoes

1 teaspoon lemon rind, grated

80 ml (2½ fl oz/⅓ cup) lemon juice, reserving the pips and skin of 1 lemon

1.2 kg (9 oz/5 cups) warmed sugar

Put two small plates in the freezer for testing purposes (you may not need the second plate). Remove the skin and tough eyes from the pineapple. Cut pineapple into quarters lengthways, remove the core and cut the flesh into 1 cm (½ inch) pieces. Peel the mango and cut each mango cheek from the stone. Cut into 1 cm (½ inch) pieces. Place the pineapple, mango, any juices, lemon rind and juice, and sugar in a large pan and stir for 5 minutes, or until all the sugar has dissolved.

Place reserved pips and skin on a square of muslin (cheesecloth), tie securely with string and add to the pan.

Bring to the boil, then reduce the heat and simmer, stirring often, for 30–40 minutes, or until setting point is reached. Remove any scum during cooking with a skimmer or slotted spoon. Stir across the base of the pan to check that the jam is not sticking or burning. Be careful because the jam will froth. When jam falls from a tilted wooden spoon in thick sheets without dripping, start testing for setting point.

Remove from the heat, place a little jam on one of the cold plates and place in the freezer for 30 seconds. A skin will form on the surface and the jam will wrinkle when pushed with your finger when setting point is reached. Remove any scum from the surface.

Pour immediately into clean, warm jars and seal. Turn upside down for 2 minutes, then invert and cool. Label and date. Store in a cool, dark place for 6–12 months. Refrigerate after opening for up to 6 weeks.

preparation 30 minutes ✦ cooking 45 minutes

Blackberry and apple jam

INGREDIENTS
750 g (1 lb 10 oz) green apples
1 kg (2 lb/7½ cups) blackberries
1.5 kg (3 lb/6½ cups) sugar, warmed

Put two small plates in the freezer for testing purposes (you may not need the second plate). Peel, core and chop the apples. Place apple pieces in a large pan with the berries and 125 ml (4 fl oz/½ cup) water. Cook, covered, over medium heat, stirring often, for 30 minutes, or until the fruit has softened.

Add the sugar and stir, without boiling, for 5 minutes, or until all the sugar has dissolved.

Bring the jam to the boil and boil for 20 minutes, stirring often. Stir across the base of the pan to check that the jam is not sticking or burning. When the jam falls from a tilted wooden spoon in thick sheets without dripping, start testing for setting point.

Remove from the heat, place a little jam onto one of the cold plates and place in the freezer for 30 seconds. A skin will form on the surface and the jam will wrinkle when pushed with your finger when setting point is reached. Remove any scum from the surface with a skimmer or slotted spoon.

Transfer to a heatproof jug and immediately pour into clean, warm jars, and seal. Turn upside down for 2 minutes, then invert and leave to cool. Label and date. Store in a cool, dark place for 6–12 months. Refrigerate after opening for up to 6 weeks.

preparation 20 minutes ✦ cooking 55 minutes

Melon and lemon conserve

INGREDIENTS

2.5 kg (5 lb 8 oz) honeydew melons
6 lemons
1 tablespoon brandy
1.25 kg (2 lb 12 oz/5½ cups) sugar, warmed

Put two small plates in the freezer for testing purposes (you may not need the second plate). Peel and seed the melons. Cut into 1 cm (½ inch) cubes and add to a large pan.

Scrub the lemons under hot, running water with a soft bristle brush to remove the wax coating, then cut them in half. Juice the lemons, retaining the pips, and add the juice to the pan. Roughly chop the lemons and divide the pieces and the pips between two squares of muslin (cheesecloth). Tie securely with string and add to the pan along with the brandy and 750 ml (25 fl oz/3 cups) water. Bring to the boil and boil for 40 minutes, or until the fruit is soft.

Add the sugar and stir over low heat, without boiling, for 5 minutes, or until all the sugar has dissolved. Bring to the boil and boil, stirring often, for 30 minutes. As the mixture thickens and starts to darken, reduce the heat and simmer, stirring frequently, for 20–30 minutes. When the conserve falls from a tilted wooden spoon in thick sheets without dripping, start testing for setting point.

Remove from the heat, place a little conserve on one cold plate and place in the freezer for 30 seconds. A skin will form on the surface and the conserve will wrinkle when pushed with your finger when setting point is reached. Discard the muslin bags. Remove any scum from the surface.

Spoon immediately into clean, warm jars and seal. Turn jars upside down for 2 minutes, then invert and leave to cool. Label and date. Store jars in a cool, dark place for 6–12 months. Refrigerate after opening for up to 6 weeks.

preparation 25 minutes * cooking 1 hour 45 minutes

Black cherry jam

INGREDIENTS

1 kg (2 lb 4 oz/about 3 cups) fresh black cherries
125 ml (4 fl oz/½ cup) lemon juice
750 g (1 lb 10 oz/3 cups) sugar, warmed
25 g (1 oz) jam-setting mixture, if required

Put two small plates in the freezer. Remove the stalks from the cherries and, using a small sharp knife, cut the cherries open and remove the pips. Alternatively, use a cherry pitter, available from kitchenware stores. Place the pips on a square of muslin (cheesecloth) and tie securely with string.

Place the cherries and muslin bag in a large pan together with 250 ml (9 fl oz/1 cup) water and the lemon juice. Bring to the boil, then reduce the heat and simmer, stirring often, for 30 minutes, or until the cherries are tender. Discard the muslin bag.

Add the sugar and stir over low heat, without boiling, for 5 minutes, or until all the sugar has dissolved. Return mixture to the boil and boil for 15–20 minutes, stirring often. Remove any scum with a skimmer or slotted spoon.

Remove from the heat, place a little jam on one of the cold plates and place in the freezer for 30 seconds. A skin will form on the surface and the jam will wrinkle when pushed with your finger when setting point is reached. If the jam doesn't set, add the jam-setting mixture, return to the heat and boil rapidly for 5 minutes. Remove any scum from the surface. Spoon immediately into clean, warm jars and seal. Turn the jars upside down for 2 minutes, then invert and leave to cool. Label and date. Store in a cool, dark place for 6–12 months. Refrigerate after opening for up to 6 weeks.

note CHERRIES ARE LOW IN PECTIN AND JAM-SETTING MIXTURE IS OFTEN ADDED. IF IT IS UNAVAILABLE, BOIL THE JAM FOR A LITTLE LONGER AND ADD MORE LEMON JUICE.

preparation 20 minutes * cooking 1 hour

Spiced dried peach conserve

INGREDIENTS

400 g (13 oz) dried peaches, cut into 2 or 3 pieces
2 cinnamon sticks
3 cloves
3 cardamom pods
1.25 kg (2 lb 12 oz/5½ cups) sugar, warmed
60 ml (2 fl oz/¼ cup) lemon juice

Place the dried peaches in a non-metallic bowl, add 1.75 litres (7 cups) water, cover and soak overnight.

Put two small plates in the freezer for testing purposes (you may not need the second plate). Pour the peaches and water into a large pan. Place the spices on a square of muslin (cheesecloth) and tie securely with string. Add to the pan with 250 ml (9 fl oz/1 cup) water. Bring to the boil, then reduce the heat and simmer for 20 minutes, or until the fruit is soft.

Add the sugar and lemon juice and stir over low heat, without boiling, for 5 minutes, or until all the sugar has dissolved. Return to the boil and boil for 20–25 minutes, stirring often. Remove any scum from the surface during cooking with a skimmer or slotted spoon. When the conserve falls from a tilted wooden spoon in thick sheets without dripping, start testing for setting point.

Remove from heat, place a little conserve on one of the cold plates and place in the freezer for 30 seconds. A skin will form on the surface and the conserve will wrinkle when pushed with your finger when setting point is reached. Discard the muslin bag. Remove any scum from the surface.

Spoon immediately into clean, warm jars. Turn upside down for 2 minutes, then invert and leave to cool. Label and date. Store in a cool, dark place for 6–12 months. Refrigerate after opening for up to 6 weeks.

preparation 15 minutes + overnight soaking * cooking 50 minutes

Boysenberry jam

INGREDIENTS

1 kg (2 lb 4 oz/about 7½ cups) fresh boysenberries

80 ml (2½ fl oz/⅓ cup) lemon juice

1 kg (2 lb 4 oz/4⅓ cups) sugar, warmed

Put two small plates in the freezer for testing purposes (you may not need the second plate). Put the berries and lemon juice in a large pan and cook gently for 10 minutes. Add sugar, stir over low heat for 5 minutes, or until all the sugar has dissolved.

Bring to the boil and boil, stirring, for 20 minutes. Remove any scum with a skimmer or slotted spoon during cooking. When the jam falls from a tilted wooden spoon in thick sheets without dripping, start testing for setting point.

Remove from the heat, place a little jam on one of the cold plates and place in the freezer for 30 seconds. A skin will form on the surface and the jam will wrinkle when pushed with your finger when setting point is reached. Remove any scum from the surface.

Pour immediately into clean, warm jars and seal. Turn the jars upside down for 2 minutes, then invert and leave to cool. Label and date. Store in a cool, dark place for 6–12 months. Refrigerate after opening for up to 6 weeks.

note IF BOYSENBERRIES ARE NOT AVAILABLE, ANY SOFT BERRY CAN BE USED, SUCH AS MULBERRIES, RASPBERRIES OR BLACKBERRIES.

preparation 20 minutes * cooking 35 minutes

EUROPEAN AND ASIAN PEARS

European pears are classically 'pear-shaped' and have sweet, buttery, slightly 'gritty' flesh that is balanced by an amount of acid. Varieties include beurre bosc, packham's triumph and doyenne du comice. Asian pears, also called nashi (which simply means 'pear' in Japanese) are round and have very crisp, juicy, sweet flesh that is mild in flavour.

Pear and ginger conserve

INGREDIENTS

1.5 kg (3 lb) beurre bosc pears
60 ml (2 fl oz/¼ cup) lemon juice
1 teaspoon grated lemon rind
1.5 kg (3 lb) sugar, warmed
150 g (5 oz/⅔ cup) glacé ginger, finely chopped

Put two small plates in the freezer for testing purposes (you may not need the second plate). Peel, halve and core the pears. Cut the flesh into 1.5 cm (½ inch) pieces. Place the cores and seeds on a piece of muslin (cheesecloth), gather up and tie securely with string. Add to a large pan with the fruit, lemon juice and rind, and 250 ml (9 fl oz/1 cup) water.

Bring to the boil, then reduce the heat and simmer for 20–25 minutes, or until the pear is soft. Add sugar and glacé ginger and stir over low heat, without boiling, for 5–10 minutes, or until the sugar has dissolved. Return to the boil and boil for 20–25 minutes, stirring often. Remove any scum during cooking with a skimmer or slotted spoon. When the conserve falls from a tilted wooden spoon in thick sheets without dripping, start testing for setting point.

Remove from heat, place a little conserve on one of the cold plates and place in the freezer for 30 seconds. A skin will form on the surface and the conserve will wrinkle when pushed with your finger when setting point is reached. Discard the muslin bag. Remove any scum from the surface.

Spoon immediately into clean, warm jars. Turn upside down for 2 minutes, then invert and leave to cool. Label and date. Store in a cool, dark place for 6–12 months. Refrigerate after opening for up to 6 weeks.

preparation 30 minutes + cooking 1 hour

Winter fruit conserve

INGREDIENTS

1.5 kg (3 lb) firm pears, peeled and cored
1 grapefruit
1 orange
1 lemon
1.5 kg (3 lb/6 ½ cups) sugar, warmed
250 g (9 oz/2 cups) raisins
60 g (2¼ oz/½ cup) sultanas
80 ml (2½ fl oz/⅓ cup) whisky

Put the pears in a food processor. Scrub the grapefruit, orange and lemon under warm, running water with a soft bristle brush to remove the wax coating, then halve and thinly slice, removing the pips. Chop the flesh and add to food processor with any juices. Process in batches until finely chopped and pulpy. Transfer to a large non-metallic bowl. Stir in the sugar, cover and leave overnight.

Place the mixture in a large pan and bring to the boil. Reduce the heat and simmer for 45 minutes, stirring often. Remove any scum during cooking with a skimmer or slotted spoon.

Add raisins and sultanas and cook, stirring often, for 45 minutes, or until thick and pulpy. Remove from the heat and stir in the whisky.

Spoon immediately into clean, warm jars and seal. Turn the jars upside down for 2 minutes, then invert and leave to cool. Label and date. Store in a cool, dark place for 6–12 months. Refrigerate after opening for up to 6 weeks.

preparation 30 minutes + overnight soaking + cooking 1 hour 30 minutes

Quince conserve

INGREDIENTS

2 kg (4 lb) quinces (about 5)
185 ml (6 fl oz/¾ cup) lemon juice
1.5 kg (3 lb 5 oz/4⅓ cups) sugar, warmed

Put two small plates in the freezer for testing purposes (you may not need the second plate). Cut each quince into quarters then peel, core and cut into small cubes. Place fruit in a large pan with 2 litres (8 cups) water and the lemon juice. Bring slowly to the boil, then reduce the heat and simmer, covered, for 1 hour, or until the fruit is soft.

Add the sugar and stir over low heat, without boiling, for 5 minutes, or until all the sugar has dissolved.

Return to the boil and boil, stirring often, for 25 minutes. Remove any scum during cooking with a skimmer or slotted spoon. When the conserve falls from a tilted wooden spoon in thick sheets without dripping, start testing for setting point.

Remove from heat, place a little conserve on one of the cold plates and place in the freezer for 30 seconds. A skin will form on the surface and the conserve will wrinkle when pushed with your finger when setting point is reached. Remove any scum from the surface with a skimmer or slotted spoon.

Spoon immediately into clean, warm jars and seal. Turn the jars upside down for 2 minutes, then invert and leave to cool. Label and date. Store in a cool, dark place for 6–12 months. Refrigerate after opening for up to 6 weeks.

note QUINCES WILL TURN FROM THEIR NATURAL YELLOW TO A BEAUTIFUL, RICH RED DURING COOKING.

preparation 20 minutes ✦ cooking 1 hour 30 minutes

Quince
Conserve

Dried apricot jam

INGREDIENTS

500 g (1 lb) dried apricots
1.5 kg (3 lb 5 oz/6½ cups) sugar, warmed
45 g (1¾ oz/½ cup) flaked almonds

Place the dried apricots in a large non-metallic bowl. Add 2 litres (8 cups) water and leave to soak overnight.

Put two small plates in the freezer for testing purposes (you may not need the second plate). Pour the apricots and the water into a large pan. Bring to the boil, then reduce heat and simmer, covered, for 45 minutes, or until the fruit is soft.

Add the sugar and stir over low heat, without boiling, for 5 minutes, or until all the sugar has dissolved. Return to the boil and boil, stirring often, for 20–25 minutes. Remove any scum during cooking with a skimmer or slotted spoon. Stir frequently across the base of the pan to prevent the jam from sticking. When the jam falls from a tilted wooden spoon in thick sheets without dripping, start testing for setting point.

Remove from the heat, place a little jam on one of the cold plates and place in the freezer for 30 seconds. A skin will form on the surface and the jam will wrinkle when pushed with your finger when setting point is reached. Remove any scum. Add the flaked almonds.

Spoon immediately into clean, warm jars and seal. Turn upside down for 2 minutes, then invert and leave to cool. Label and date. Store in a cool, dark place for 6–12 months. Refrigerate after opening for up to 6 weeks.

preparation 10 minutes + overnight soaking * cooking 1 hour 10 minutes

PIKELETS WITH JAM

125 g (4½ oz/1 cup) self-raising flour
1 tablespoon caster (superfine) sugar
185 ml (6 fl oz/¾ cup) milk
1 egg
jam, to serve

Sift the flour, sugar and a pinch of salt into a large bowl and make a well in the centre. Whisk the milk and egg in a jug and slowly pour into the well, whisking to form a smooth batter.

Heat a non-stick frying pan (skillet) over medium heat and brush lightly with melted butter or oil.

Drop level tablespoons of batter into the frying pan, allowing room for spreading (you will probably fit about four pikelets in the pan at a time). Cook the pikelets for about 30 seconds, or until small bubbles begin to appear on the surface and the underneath has turned golden brown. Turn pikelets over; cook the other side.

Transfer to a plate or wire rack to cool, and repeat with the remaining batter. Serve the pikelets topped with jam, and with whipped cream if desired.

PREPARATION 10 MINUTES
COOKING 15 MINUTES
MAKES ABOUT 25 PIKELETS

Tomato and passionfruit jam

INGREDIENTS

2 kg (4 lb 8 oz) tomatoes

250 g (9 oz/1 cup) passionfruit pulp (about 10 passionfruit)

60 ml (2 fl oz/¼ cup) lemon juice

2.5 kg (5 lb 8 oz/10¾ cups) sugar, warmed

Put two small plates in the freezer for testing purposes (you may not need the second plate). Cut a cross at the base of each tomato, place tomatoes in a large bowl, cover with boiling water and leave for about 30 seconds, or until the skins start to peel away. Transfer to a bowl of icy cold water, remove the skins and roughly chop the flesh.

Put the passionfruit pulp, lemon juice, tomato and any juices in a large pan. Bring to the boil, then reduce the heat and simmer for 15 minutes, or until thick and pulpy.

Add the sugar and stir over low heat, without boiling, until all the sugar has dissolved. Return to the boil and boil for 30–40 minutes, stirring often. Remove any scum during cooking with a skimmer or slotted spoon. When the jam falls from a tilted wooden spoon in thick sheets without dripping, start testing for setting point.

Remove from the heat, place a little jam onto one of the cold plates and place in the freezer for 30 seconds. A skin will form on the surface and the jam will wrinkle when pushed with your finger when setting point is reached. Remove any scum from the surface.

Pour immediately into clean, warm jars, and seal. Turn jars upside down for 2 minutes, then invert and leave to cool. Label and date. Store in a cool, dark place for 6–12 months. Refrigerate after opening for up to 6 weeks.

preparation 25 minutes * cooking 1 hour

Fig and orange jam

INGREDIENTS

1.5 kg (3 lb) fresh figs, chopped
185 ml (6 fl oz/¾ cup) orange juice
60 ml (2 fl oz/¼ cup) lemon juice
2 tablespoons sweet sherry
1 kg (2 lb 4 oz/4⅓ cups) sugar, warmed

Put two small plates in the freezer for testing purposes (you may not need the second plate). Place the figs in a large pan with the orange and lemon juice, and the sherry. Bring to the boil, then reduce the heat and simmer for 20 minutes, or until the figs are soft.

Add the sugar and stir over low heat, without boiling, until all the sugar has dissolved. Return to the boil and boil for 20–25 minutes, stirring often. Remove any scum during cooking with a skimmer or slotted spoon. When the jam falls from a tilted wooden spoon in thick sheets without dripping, start testing for setting point.

Remove from the heat, place a little jam on one of the cold plates and place in the freezer for 30 seconds. A skin will form on the surface and the jam will wrinkle when pushed with your finger when setting point is reached. Remove any scum from the surface with a skimmer or slotted spoon.

Pour immediately into clean, warm jars and seal. Turn jars upside down for 2 minutes, then invert and leave to cool. Label and date. Store in a cool, dark place for 6–12 months. Refrigerate after opening for up to 6 weeks.

note EITHER DARK- OR GREEN-SKINNED FIGS CAN BE USED IN THIS RECIPE.

preparation 20 minutes ✦ cooking 50 minutes

MARMALADES AND JELLIES

Redcurrant jelly

INGREDIENTS

600 g (1 lb 4 oz/about 5 cups) redcurrants

600 g (1 lb 4 oz/2¾ cups) caster (superfine) sugar, warmed

Put two small plates in the freezer for testing purposes (you may not need the second plate). Place the redcurrants, including stems, and sugar in a pan. Crush the redcurrants to release the juices. Cook, stirring, over low heat, until all the sugar has dissolved.

Increase the heat and boil rapidly for 5 minutes, stirring often. Remove from the heat, place a little jelly on one of the cold plates and place in the freezer for 30 seconds. When setting point is reached, a skin will form on the surface and the jelly will wrinkle when pushed with your finger. Skim off any scum with a skimmer or slotted spoon and push the mixture through a fine sieve into a heatproof jug.

Pour immediately into clean, warm jars and seal. Turn the jars upside down for 2 minutes, then invert and leave to cool. Label and date. Store in a cool, dark place for 6–12 months. Refrigerate jars after opening for up to 6 weeks.

note FOR A SHINY GLAZE AND BEAUTIFUL FINISH ON SWEET FRUIT TARTS, MELT A LITTLE JELLY WITH WATER AND BRUSH OVER THE TOP OF THE FRUIT. OR MELT A SPOONFUL IN SAVOURY SAUCES AND GRAVIES.

preparation 20 minutes ✦ cooking 20 minutes

Roast turkey *with redcurrant jelly*

For celebratory occasions, a roast turkey with all the trimmings is the perfect meal and the effort and time that goes into its preparation will be well rewarded with praise.

INGREDIENTS

3 kg (6 lb 12 oz) turkey
300 g (10½ oz) butter, softened
1 onion, roughly chopped
4 sage leaves
1 rosemary sprig
½ celery stalk, cut into 2–3 pieces
1 carrot, cut into 3–4 pieces
250 ml (9 fl oz/1 cup) dry white wine
125 ml (4 fl oz/½ cup) dry marsala
250 ml (9 fl oz/1 cup) chicken stock
redcurrant jelly (recipe on previous page)

STUFFING

100 g (3½ oz) prosciutto, finely chopped
220 g (8 oz) minced (ground) pork
220 g (8 oz) minced (ground) chicken
1 egg
90 ml (3 fl oz) thick (double/heavy) cream
175 g (6 oz/⅓ cup) chestnut purée
½ teaspoon finely chopped fresh sage
a pinch of cayenne pepper

Preheat the oven to 170°C (325°F/Gas 3). Combine all the stuffing ingredients in a bowl, season well with sea salt and freshly ground black pepper and mix thoroughly.

Fill the turkey with the stuffing and sew up the opening with kitchen string. Cross the legs and tie them together, then tuck the wings behind the body. Rub the skin with 100 g (3½ oz) of the butter. Put onion in the centre of a large roasting tin and place the turkey on top, breast side up. Add another 100 g (3½ oz) of butter to the tin with the sage, rosemary, celery and carrot, then pour the wine and marsala over.

Roast for 2½–3 hours, basting several times with the pan juices and covering the turkey breast with buttered baking paper when the skin becomes golden brown. Transfer the turkey to a large warmed plate, cover loosely with foil and leave to rest in a warm place for 30 minutes before carving.

Transfer the vegetables to a food processor and blend until smooth. Add the pan juices and any scrapings from the base of the tin and process until well blended. Transfer to a saucepan, add the remaining butter and stock and bring to the boil. Season and cook until thickened, then transfer to a gravy boat.

Serve the turkey with the stuffing, gravy and redcurrant jelly.

preparation approximately 40 minutes * cooking 2½-3 hours + 30 minutes resting time before serving * serves 8

Quince jelly

INGREDIENTS

2 kg (4 lb 8 oz) ripe yellow quinces
60 ml (2 fl oz/¼ cup) lemon juice
750 g (1 lb 10 oz/3 cups) caster (superfine) sugar, warmed

Wipe the quinces clean, then cut into 5 cm (2 inch) pieces, including the skin and cores. Place the quince pieces in a large pan with 2 litres (8 cups) water. Bring slowly to the boil, then reduce the heat and simmer, covered, for 1 hour, or until tender. Mash any firmer pieces with a potato masher.

Place a jelly bag in a bowl, cover with boiling water, drain and suspend the bag over a large heatproof bowl.

Ladle fruit and liquid into the bag. Do not push the fruit through the bag or the jelly will become cloudy. Cover the top of the bag loosely with a clean tea towel (dish towel), without touching the fruit mixture. Allow the mixture to drip through the bag overnight, or until there is no liquid dripping through the cloth.

Put two small plates in the freezer for testing purposes (you may not need the second plate). Discard the pulp and measure the liquid. Pour liquid into a large pan and stir in the lemon juice. Add 250 g (9 oz/1 cup) of the warmed sugar for each 250 ml (9 fl oz/1 cup) of liquid. Stir over low heat for 5 minutes, or until all the sugar has dissolved. Bring to the boil and boil rapidly for 20–25 minutes, stirring often. Skim any scum during cooking with a skimmer or slotted spoon. Start testing for setting point.

Remove from the heat, place a little jelly on one of the cold plates and place in the freezer for 30 seconds. When setting point is reached, a skin will form on the surface and the jelly will wrinkle when pushed with your finger. Remove any scum.

Pour immediately into clean, warm jars; seal. Turn upside down for 2 minutes, then invert and leave to cool. Label and date. Store in a cool, dark place for 6–12 months. Refrigerate after opening for up to 6 weeks.

preparation 20 minutes + overnight draining ✦ cooking 1 hour 30 minutes

Three-fruit marmalade

INGREDIENTS
1 grapefruit
2 oranges
2 lemons
3 kg (6 lb 12 oz/13 cups) sugar, warmed

Scrub fruit under warm, running water with a soft bristle brush to remove wax coating. Quarter grapefruit and halve the oranges and lemons, slice them thinly and place in a non-metallic bowl. Retain the pips and place them on a square of muslin (cheesecloth) and tie securely with string. Add the muslin bag to the bowl with 2.5 litres (10 cups) water, cover and leave overnight.

Put two small plates in the freezer for testing purposes (you may not need the second plate). Put the fruit and water in a large pan. Bring to the boil, then reduce the heat and simmer, covered, for 1 hour, or until the fruit is tender.

Add the sugar and stir over low heat, without boiling, for 5 minutes, or until all the sugar has dissolved. Return to the boil and boil rapidly for 50–60 minutes, stirring often. Remove any scum during cooking with a skimmer or slotted spoon. When the marmalade falls from a tilted wooden spoon in thick sheets without dripping, start testing for setting point.

Remove from heat, place a little marmalade on one of the cold plates and place in the freezer for30 seconds. When setting point is reached, a skin will form on the surface and the marmalade will wrinkle when it is pushed with your finger. Discard the muslin bag. Remove any scum from the surface.

Spoon immediately into clean, warm jars, and seal. Turn the jars upside down for 2 minutes, then invert and leave to cool. Label and date. Store in a cool, dark place for 6–12 months. Refrigerate after opening for up to 6 weeks.

preparation 30 minutes + overnight soaking ✦ cooking 2 hours 5 minutes

PINDER BROTHERS
SHEFFIELD

Seville orange marmalade

INGREDIENTS

4 Seville oranges (about 1.25 kg/2½ lb)
2–2.25 kg (4–4½ lb) sugar, warmed

Scrub oranges under warm, running water with a soft bristle brush to remove any wax coating. Cut the oranges in half, and then in half again. Slice the oranges thinly, removing and retaining the pips. Place pips on a square of muslin (cheesecloth) and tie securely with a piece of string. Place the oranges and the muslin bag in a large non-metallic bowl. Cover the fruit and pips with 2 litres (8 cups) water and leave overnight.

Put two small plates in the freezer for testing purposes (you may not need the second plate). Place fruit and muslin bag in a large pan. Bring slowly to the boil, reduce heat and simmer, covered, for 45 minutes, or until the fruit is tender.

Measure fruit and for every 250 ml (9 fl oz/1 cup) of the fruit mixture add 250 g (9 oz/1 cup) of warmed sugar. Stir over low heat, without boiling, for 5 minutes, or until all the sugar has dissolved. Return to the boil and boil rapidly for 30–40 minutes, stirring often. Remove scum during cooking with a skimmer or slotted spoon. When marmalade falls from a tilted wooden spoon in thick sheets without dripping, start testing for setting point. Remove from the heat, place a little marmalade on one of the cold plates and place in the freezer for 30 seconds. When setting point is reached, a skin will form on the surface and marmalade will wrinkle when pushed with your finger. Discard muslin bag. Remove any scum from the surface. Spoon immediately into clean, warm jars and seal. Turn upside down for 2 minutes, then invert and cool. Label and date. Store in a cool, dark place for 6–12 months. Refrigerate after opening for up to 6 weeks.

note SEVILLE ORANGES ARE TROPICAL OR SEMI-TROPICAL FRUITS THAT MAKE GREAT MARMALADE DUE TO THEIR THICK, ROUGH SKIN AND TART FLESH. THEY ARE GENERALLY ONLY USED IN COOKING.

preparation 30 minutes + overnight soaking ✦ cooking 1 hour 30 minutes

Grape jelly

INGREDIENTS

2 kg (4 lb 8 oz/about 10 cups) black seedless grapes
80 ml (2½ fl oz/⅓ cup) lemon juice, reserving any pips
560 g (1 lb 4 oz/2¼ cups) sugar, warmed

Remove the stems from the grapes. Place the grapes in a large pan and add 250 ml (9 fl oz/1 cup) water. Place lemon pips on a square of muslin (cheesecloth) and tie securely with string. Add to pan. Slowly bring to the boil, then reduce heat and simmer for 30–35 minutes, or until grapes are soft and pulpy. Remove and discard the muslin bag.

Place a jelly bag in a bowl, cover with boiling water, drain and suspend the bag over a large heatproof bowl.

Ladle grape mixture into the jelly bag. Do not push the fruit through the bag or the jelly will turn cloudy. Cover the top of the bag loosely with a clean tea towel (dish towel), without touching the fruit mixture. Allow mixture to drip through the bag overnight, or until no liquid drips through the cloth.

Discard the pulp and measure the liquid. Pour the liquid into a stainless steel or enamel pan and stir in the lemon juice. Add 185 g (6½ oz/¾ cup) sugar for each 250 ml (9 fl oz/1 cup) liquid. Stir over a low heat until all the sugar has dissolved, then bring to the boil and boil rapidly, stirring often, for 20–25 minutes, skimming any scum during cooking with a skimmer or slotted spoon.

Transfer to a heatproof jug and immediately pour the jelly down the insides of clean, warm jars and seal. Turn the jars upside down for 2 minutes, then invert and leave to cool. Label and date. Store in a cool, dark place for 6–12 months. Refrigerate after opening for up to 6 weeks.

preparation 15 minutes overnight draining ✦ cooking 1 hour 5 minutes

Cumquat marmalade

INGREDIENTS

1 kg (2 lb 4 oz) cumquats
60 ml (2 fl oz/¼ cup) lemon juice
1.25 kg (2 lb 12 oz) sugar, warmed

Scrub the cumquats under warm, running water with a soft bristle brush to remove the wax coating. Discard the stems. Halve each lengthways, removing and retaining the pips, and slice finely. Place pips on a square of muslin (cheesecloth) and tie securely with string. Put the fruit and pips in a large non-metallic bowl. Add 1.25 litres (5 cups) water, cover with plastic wrap and leave overnight.

Put two small plates in the freezer for testing purposes (you may not need the second plate). Place the cumquats and muslin bag in a large pan with the lemon juice. Bring slowly to the boil, then reduce the heat and simmer, covered, for 30 minutes, or until the fruit is tender.

Add the warmed sugar. Stir over low heat, without boiling, for 5 minutes, or until all the sugar has dissolved. Return the mixture to the boil and boil rapidly, stirring frequently, for 20 minutes. Skim any scum from the surface during cooking with a skimmer or slotted spoon. When the marmalade falls from a tilted wooden spoon in thick sheets without dripping, start testing for setting point.

Remove the pan from the heat, place a little marmalade on one of the cold plates and place in the freezer for 30 seconds. A skin will form on the surface and the marmalade will wrinkle when pushed with your finger when setting point is reached. Discard the muslin bag. Remove any scum from the surface.

Spoon immediately into clean, warm jars. Turn upside down for 2 minutes, then invert and leave to cool. Label and date. Store in a cool, dark place for 6–12 months. Refrigerate after opening for up to 6 weeks.

preparation 20 minutes + overnight soaking ✦ cooking 1 hour

Pomegranate jelly

INGREDIENTS

2–2.5 kg (4–5 lb) pomegranates (about 8 pomegranates)

3 green apples

about 500 g (1 lb 2 oz/2 cups) caster (superfine) sugar, warmed

60 ml (2 fl oz/¼ cup) lemon juice

Cut pomegranates in half; use a juicer to squeeze out the juice. At least 500 ml (17 fl oz/2 cups) of juice will be needed. (The amount of juice in the fruit varies and, hence, the amount of sugar needed will vary.) Chop apples; include skin and cores. Place in large pan with pomegranate juice and 250 ml (9 fl oz/1 cup) water. Bring slowly to the boil, reduce heat and simmer, covered, for 20 minutes, or until the apple is mushy.

Place a jelly bag in a large bowl, cover with boiling water, drain and suspend the bag over a large heatproof bowl. Place a large heatproof bowl under the cloth. Ladle the fruit and liquid into the bag. Do not push the fruit through the bag or the jelly will become cloudy. Cover the top of the bag loosely with a clean tea towel, without touching the fruit mixture. Allow the mixture to drip through the bag overnight, or until there is no liquid dripping through the cloth. Put two small plates in the freezer for testing purposes (you may not need the second plate). Discard pulp and measure the liquid. Pour the liquid into a large pan. Add 250 g/ (9 oz/1 cup) of sugar for every 250 ml (9 fl oz/1 cup) of the liquid and stir over medium heat until all the sugar has dissolved. Stir in lemon juice. Bring to the boil and boil rapidly for 15–20 minutes, stirring often. Skim scum off the surface with a skimmer or slotted spoon during cooking. Start testing for setting point.

Remove from the heat, place a little jelly on one of the cold plates and place in the freezer for 30 seconds. A skin will form on the surface and the jelly will wrinkle when pushed with your finger when setting point is reached. Remove any scum from the surface. Stand the clean, warm jars on a wooden board or a cloth-covered surface. Carefully transfer the jelly to a heatproof jug. Wrap the jars in a cloth to protect your hands. Tilt the jar and pour the jelly down the sides of the jars to stop bubbles forming. Seal the jars while hot and gently turn upside down for 2 minutes, then invert and leave to cool. Label and date. Store in a cool, dark place for 6–12 months. Refrigerate after opening for up to 6 weeks.

preparation 15 minutes + overnight draining ✦ cooking 50 minutes

Cointreau orange marmalade

INGREDIENTS

1 kg (2 lb 4 oz) oranges

2 kg (4 lb 8 oz/8¼ cups) sugar, warmed

80 ml (2½ fl oz/⅓ cup) Cointreau or other orange-flavoured liqueur

Scrub oranges with a soft bristle brush under warm, running water to remove the wax coating. Cut them in half, then into thin slices, reserving the pips. Place the pips on a square of muslin (cheesecloth) and tie securely with string. Place orange slices and muslin bag in a large non-metallic bowl with 2 litres (8 cups) water, cover and leave overnight.

Put two small plates in the freezer for testing purposes (you may not need the second plate). Transfer fruit, water and muslin bag to a large pan. Bring slowly to the boil, then reduce the heat and simmer, covered, for 1 hour, or until the fruit is tender and the mixture has reduced by a third.

Measure fruit and for every 250 ml (9 fl oz/1 cup) of the fruit mixture add 250 g (9 oz/1 cup) of warmed sugar. Stir over low heat, without boiling, for 5 minutes, or until all the sugar has dissolved. Bring to the boil and boil rapidly for 40–50 minutes, stirring often. Remove any scum during cooking with a skimmer or slotted spoon. When the marmalade falls from a tilted wooden spoon in thick sheets without dripping, start testing for setting point.

Remove from heat, place a little marmalade on one of the cold plates and place in freezer for 30 seconds. A skin will form on the surface and marmalade will wrinkle when pushed with your finger when setting point is reached. Discard muslin bag. Remove scum from the surface. Stir in the Cointreau.

Spoon immediately into clean, warm jars. Turn upside down for 2 minutes, then invert and leave to cool. Label and date. Store in a cool, dark place for 6–12 months. Refrigerate after opening for up to 6 weeks.

preparation 25 minutes +overnight soaking✦ cooking 2 hours

REFRESHING LIMES

There could be nothing more refreshing than the smell of a just-cut lime. Use their piquant juice to flavour drinks such as margaritas and in dishes such as quacamole and salsa. Squeeze fresh juice over papaya chunks and mango to add a bit of zing.

Lime marmalade

INGREDIENTS

1 kg (2 lb 4 oz) limes

2.25 kg (5 lb/9¾ cups) sugar, warmed

Scrub limes under warm, running water with a soft bristle brush to remove the wax coating. Cut in half lengthways, reserving pips, slice thinly and place in a large non-metallic bowl with 2 litres (8 cups) water. Tie lime pips securely in a square of muslin (cheesecloth) and add to the bowl. Cover and leave overnight.

Put two small plates in the freezer for testing purposes (you may not need the second plate). Place the fruit and water in a large pan. Bring slowly to the boil, then reduce the heat and simmer, covered, for 45 minutes, or until the fruit is tender. Add the sugar and stir over low heat, without boiling, for 5 minutes, or until all the sugar has dissolved. Return to the boil and boil rapidly, stirring often, for 20 minutes. Remove any scum during cooking with a skimmer or slotted spoon. When the marmalade falls from a tilted wooden spoon in thick sheets without dripping, start testing for setting point.

Remove from heat, place a little marmalade on one of the cold plates and place in freezer for 30 seconds. A skin will form on the surface and the marmalade will wrinkle when pushed with your finger when setting point is reached. Discard the muslin bag. Remove any scum from the surface.

Spoon immediately into clean, warm jars. Turn upside down for 2 minutes, then invert and leave to cool. Label and date. Store in a cool, dark place for 6–12 months. Refrigerate after opening for up to 6 weeks.

note LOOK FOR BRIGHTLY COLOURED LIMES THAT FEEL HEAVY FOR THEIR SIZE.

preparation 20 minutes + overnight soaking ✦ cooking 1 hour 10 minutes

Lime
Marmalade

Chicken *in tangy lime marmalade sauce*

Stir-frying is the perfect technique for the busy cook. The addition of lime marmalade in this recipe adds an intense depth of flavour to the mild-tasting chicken.

INGREDIENTS

500 g (1 lb) chicken thigh fillets, cut into strips

5 cm (2 inch) piece ginger, cut into paper-thin slices

4 spring onions, thinly sliced

oil, for cooking

1 red capsicum, thinly sliced

1 tablespoon mirin

1 tablespoon lime marmalade (recipe on previous page)

2 teaspoons grated lime rind

2 tablespoons lime juice

Put the chicken, ginger, spring onion and some ground black pepper in a dish. Toss well to combine.

Heat a wok until very hot, add 1 tablespoon of the oil and swirl it around to coat the side. Stir-fry chicken mixture in three batches over high heat for about 3 minutes, or until golden brown and cooked through. Reheat the wok in between each batch, adding more oil when necessary. Remove all the chicken from the wok and set aside.

Reheat wok, add the capsicum and stir-fry for 30 seconds. Add the mirin, marmalade, lime rind and juice, and season with salt and freshly ground black pepper. Cover and steam for 1 minute. Add the chicken and cook, uncovered, for 2 minutes, or until heated through.

Hint CHOOSE YOUNG GINGER WITH THIN SKIN AS IT WILL BE TENDER AND EASY TO SLICE.

preparation 25 minutes ✦ cooking 20 minutes ✦ serves 4

Grapefruit marmalade

INGREDIENTS
1.25 kg (2 lb 12 oz) grapefruit (about 3 large)
2 lemons
2.5 kg (5 lb 8 oz/11 cups) sugar, warmed

Scrub fruit under warm, running water with a soft bristle brush to remove the wax coating. Remove the rind from the fruit in long strips, avoiding the bitter white pith. Cut the strips into 5 cm (2 inch) lengths, then slice thinly. Remove the white pith from the fruit, then chop the flesh, discarding the pips. Place all the fruit and rind in a large non-metallic bowl with 2.5 litres (10 cups) water; cover, leave overnight.

Put two small plates in the freezer for testing purposes (you may not need the second plate). Place fruit and water in a large pan, bring to the boil, then reduce heat and simmer, covered, for 45 minutes, or until the fruit is tender.

Add the sugar and stir over low heat, without boiling, for 5 minutes, or until all the sugar has dissolved. Return to the boil and boil, stirring often, for 40–50 minutes, checking frequently in the last 20 minutes. Remove any scum during cooking with a skimmer or slotted spoon. When the marmalade falls from a tilted wooden spoon in thick sheets without dripping, start testing for setting point.

Remove from the heat, place a little marmalade on one of the cold plates and place in the freezer for 30 seconds. A skin will form on the surface and the marmalade will wrinkle when pushed with your finger when setting point is reached. Remove any scum from the surface with a skimmer or slotted spoon.

Spoon immediately into clean, warm jars and seal. Turn the jars upside down for 2 minutes, then invert and leave to cool. Label and date. Store in a cool, dark place for 6–12 months. Refrigerate after opening for up to 6 weeks.

preparation 30 minutes + overnight soaking ✦ cooking 1 hour 40 minutes

GRAPEFRUIT

The grapefruit is the largest known citrus and is named for the fact that it grows in heavy grapelike clusters. When buying grapefruit, you'll see that they are classified as white, pink or ruby, which refers to the colour of their flesh and not their skin. Choose fruit that feel heavy for their size.

Apple and rose jelly

INGREDIENTS

1.5 kg (3 lb 5 oz) apples

2 unsprayed roses

about 300 g (10 oz/1⅓ cups) caster (superfine) sugar, warmed

2 teaspoons rosewater

Chop the apples and put them in a pan with 1 litre (4 cups) water. Cook over a low heat for 45 minutes, or until the apples have broken down into a purée. Place a jelly bag in a bowl, cover with boiling water, drain and suspend the bag over a large heatproof bowl.

Ladle purée into the bag. Do not push the fruit through the bag or the jelly will become cloudy. Cover the top of the bag loosely with a clean tea towel (dish towel), without touching the fruit mixture. Allow mixture to drip through the bag overnight, or until there is no liquid dripping through the cloth.

Put two small plates in the freezer for testing purposes (you may not need the second plate). Pull the petals off the roses and wash them gently in cold water. Discard the pulp and measure the liquid. Pour the liquid into a large pan and add 310 g (11 oz/1⅓ cups) warmed sugar for every 600 ml (21 fl oz/2½ cups) liquid. Stir over a low heat until all the sugar has dissolved. Bring to the boil and boil, stirring mixture frequently, for 5–10 minutes. Skim off any scum during cooking with a slotted spoon. Start testing for setting point.

Remove from the heat, place a little jelly on one of the cold plates and place in the freezer for 30 seconds. A skin will form on the surface and the jelly will wrinkle when pushed with your finger when setting point is reached. Remove any scum from the surface. Stir in rose petals and rosewater, then leave to cool slightly until the jelly is beginning to set (this will ensure that the rose petals are suspended in the jelly).

Pour the jelly down the sides of clean, warm jars and seal. Turn the jars upside down for 10 minutes, then slowly invert them to disperse the petals evenly. Label and date. Store in a cool, dark place for 6–12 months. Refrigerate after opening for up to 6 weeks.

preparation 20 minutes + overnight draining ✦ cooking 1 hour

SAVOURY JAMS AND PICKLES

Onion and thyme marmalade

INGREDIENTS

2 kg (4 lb 8 oz) onions, cut into rings
750 ml (26 fl oz/3 cups) malt vinegar
6 black peppercorns
2 bay leaves
805 g (1 lb 2 oz/3½ cups) firmly packed soft brown sugar
2 tablespoons fresh thyme leaves
10 x 3 cm (1¼ inch) sprigs fresh thyme

Place the onion in a large pan with the vinegar. Put the peppercorns and bay leaves on a square of muslin (cheesecloth) and tie securely with string. Add to the pan. Bring to the boil, then reduce the heat and simmer for 40–45 minutes, or until the onion is very soft.

Add sugar, thyme leaves and 1 teaspoon salt. Stir until all the sugar has dissolved. Bring to the boil, then reduce the heat and simmer, for 20–30 minutes, or until thick and syrupy. Skim any scum off the surface during cooking with a skimmer or slotted spoon. Discard the muslin bag and stir in the fresh thyme sprigs.

Spoon the onion pulp immediately into clean, warm jars, then pour in the syrup and seal the jars. Turn the jars upside down for 2 minutes, then invert and leave to cool. Label and date. Leave for 1 month before opening to allow the flavours to develop. Store in a cool, dark place for up to 12 months. Refrigerate after opening for up to 6 weeks.

preparation 20 minutes * cooking 1 hour 20 minutes

Roast lamb *with onion and thyme marmalade*

Rosemary and lamb are one of the great flavour combinations. Thyme, another resinous herb, makes a great addition to the roast when included in an onion marmalade.

INGREDIENTS

2 rosemary sprigs
3 garlic cloves, chopped
75 g (2½ oz) pancetta, chopped
2 kg (4 lb 8 oz) leg of lamb, shank bone cut off just above joint, trimmed of excess fat and tied
1 large onion
125 ml (4 fl oz/½ cup) olive oil
375 ml (13 fl oz/1½ cups) dry white wine
onion and thyme marmalade (see previous page)

Preheat the oven to 230°C (450°F/Gas 8). Pull the leaves off the rosemary sprigs. Using a large, sharp knife, chop rosemary, garlic and pancetta until a coarse paste forms, then season with sea salt and freshly ground black pepper. Using a small, sharp knife, make incisions 1 cm (½ inch) deep all over the lamb. Then rub the rosemary mixture over the lamb, pushing it into the incisions.

Peel the onion, then cut it widthways into four thick slices and place in the centre of a roasting tin. Sit the lamb leg on top, pour the olive oil over, then roast for 15 minutes.

Reduce the oven temperature to 180°C (350°F/Gas 4) and pour in 250 ml (9 fl oz/1 cup) of the wine. Roast for 1¼ hours for medium–rare, or until cooked to your liking, basting from time to time and adding a little water if the juices start to burn. Transfer the lamb leg to a warm platter, cover loosely with foil and leave to rest in a warm place for 10 minutes.

Remove the onion from the roasting tin and spoon off the excess fat. Place the tin over high heat on the stovetop, pour in the remaining wine and cook for 3–4 minutes, or until the sauce reduces and thickens. Season to taste. Carve the lamb. Arrange on warmed plates and serve with the spooned sauce over the top and with onion and thyme marmalade on the side.

preparation 20 minutes ✦ cooking 1 hour 45 minutes ✦ serves 6

Tomato sauce

INGREDIENTS

2.5 kg (5 lb 8 oz) firm, ripe tomatoes
1 large onion
2 teaspoons black peppercorns
2 teaspoons whole cloves
2 teaspoons whole allspice (pimento)
1½ tablespoons tomato paste (purée)
4 cloves garlic, crushed
2 teaspoons ground ginger
¼ teaspoon cayenne pepper
600 ml (21 fl oz/2½ cups) white wine or cider vinegar
250 g (9 oz/1 cup) sugar

Roughly chop the tomatoes and onion. Place the peppercorns, whole cloves and allspice on a square of muslin (cheesecloth) and tie securely with string.

Place the tomato and onion in a large pan with the muslin bag, tomato paste, garlic, ginger, cayenne pepper, vinegar and 1 teaspoon salt. Bring slowly to the boil, reduce the heat and simmer for 45 minutes. Add the sugar and stir over low heat for 5 minutes, or until all the sugar has dissolved. Bring to the boil, then reduce the heat and simmer for 1 hour, or until the sauce is thick and pulpy. Stir frequently during cooking and watch that the mixture does not burn. Discard the muslin bag.

Place the mixture in a coarse sieve set over a large bowl, in batches if necessary. Use a metal spoon to press all the juices firmly from the pulp. Discard the pulp and return the juice to the clean pan. Gently reheat the mixture for 10 minutes, then pour immediately into clean, warm jars or bottles and seal. Turn jars upside down for 2 minutes, then invert them and leave to cool. Label and date. Leave for 1 month before opening to allow the flavours to develop. Store in a cool, dark place for up to 12 months. Refrigerate after opening for up to 6 weeks.

preparation 25 minutes ✦ cooking 2 hours

Sausage rolls *with tomato sauce*

A firm favourite in lunchboxes, as party fare or as a meal with a salad, every good sausage roll deserves a dollop of top-quality tomato sauce.

INGREDIENTS

3 sheets frozen puff pastry, thawed
2 eggs, lightly beaten
750 g (1 lb 10 oz) minced (ground) sausage
1 onion, finely chopped
1 garlic clove, crushed
80 g (2¾ oz/1 cup) fresh breadcrumbs
3 tablespoons chopped flat-leaf (Italian) parsley
3 tablespoons chopped thyme
½ teaspoon ground sage
½ teaspoon freshly grated nutmeg
½ teaspoon ground cloves
tomato sauce (recipe on previous page)

Preheat the oven to 200°C (400°F/Gas 6). Lightly grease two baking trays.

Cut the pastry sheets in half and lightly brush the edges with some of the beaten egg.

Mix half the remaining egg with the remaining ingredients and ½ teaspoon black pepper in a large bowl, then divide into 6 even portions. Pipe or spoon the filling down the centre of each piece of pastry, then brush the edges with some of the egg. Fold the pastry over the filling, overlapping the edges and placing the join underneath. Brush the rolls with more egg, then cut each into six short pieces.

Cut two small slashes on top of each roll, place on the baking trays and bake for 15 minutes. Reduce the heat to 180°C (350°F/Gas 4) and bake for another 15 minutes, or until puffed and golden. Place tomato sauce in a jug and serve alongside.

preparation 30 minutes ✦ cooking 30 minutes ✦ makes 36

Preserved lemons

INGREDIENTS

8–12 small thin-skinned lemons

315 g (11 oz/1 cup) rock salt

500 ml (17 fl oz/2 cups) lemon juice (8–10 lemons)

½ teaspoon black peppercorns

1 bay leaf

1 tablespoon olive oil

Scrub the lemons under warm running water with a soft bristle brush to remove the wax coating. Cut into quarters, leaving the base attached at the stem end. Gently open each lemon, remove any visible pips and pack 1 tablespoon of the salt against the cut edges of each lemon. Push the lemons back into shape and pack tightly into a 2 litre (8 cup) jar with a clip or tight-fitting lid. (Depending on the size of the lemons, you may not need all 12. They should be firmly packed and fill the jar.)

Add 250 ml (9 fl oz/1 cup) of the lemon juice, the remaining rock salt, the peppercorns and bay leaf to the jar. Fill the jar to the top with the remaining lemon juice. Seal and shake to combine all the ingredients. Leave in a cool, dark place for 6 weeks, inverting each week. (In warm weather, store in the refrigerator.) The liquid will be cloudy initially, but will clear by the fourth week.

To test if the lemons are preserved, cut through the centre of one of the lemon quarters. If the pith is still white, the lemons are not ready. Re-seal and leave for another week before testing again.

Once the lemons are preserved, cover the brine with a layer of olive oil. Replace the oil each time you remove some of the lemon.

note SERVE THE LEMONS WITH GRILLED MEATS OR USE TO FLAVOUR COUSCOUS, STUFFINGS, TAGINES AND CASSEROLES. ONLY THE RIND IS USED IN COOKING. DISCARD THE FLESH, RINSE AND FINELY SLICE OR CHOP THE RIND BEFORE ADDING TO THE DISH.

preparation 1 hour + 6 weeks standing * no cooking required

Chicken with olives *and preserved lemons*

This is one of the classic dishes of Morocco, where preserved lemons are frequently used. Use unpitted olives; if bitter, blanch in boiling water for 5 minutes before use.

INGREDIENTS

60 ml (2 fl oz/¼ cup) olive oil
1.6 kg (3 lb 8 oz) chicken
1 onion, chopped
2 garlic cloves, chopped
625 ml (21½ fl oz/2½ cups) chicken stock
½ teaspoon ground ginger
1½ teaspoons ground cinnamon
pinch saffron threads
100 g (3½ oz) green olives
¼ preserved lemon, pulp removed, zest washed and cut into slivers
2 bay leaves
2 chicken livers
3 tablespoons chopped coriander (cilantro) leaves

Preheat the oven to 180°C (350°F/Gas 4). Heat 2 tablespoons of the oil in a large frying pan, add the chicken and brown on all sides. Place in a deep flameproof casserole dish. Heat the remaining oil in the pan, add the onion and garlic and cook over medium heat for 3–4 minutes, or until softened. Add the stock, ginger, cinnamon, saffron, olives, lemon and bay leaves and pour around the chicken. Bake for 45 minutes, or until the juices run clear when the thigh is pierced with a skewer, adding a little more water or stock if the sauce gets too dry.

Remove the chicken from the casserole dish, cover with foil and leave to rest. Put the dish on the stovetop over medium heat, add the chicken livers and mash into the sauce as they cook. Cook for 5–6 minutes, or until the sauce has reduced and thickened. Add the chopped coriander. Cut the chicken into four pieces and serve with the sauce.

preparation 10 minutes ✦ cooking 1 hour ✦ serves 4

Indian lime pickle

INGREDIENTS

10 firm yellow/pale green limes
185 m (6 fl oz/¾ cup) oil
1 teaspoon fenugreek seeds
¾ teaspoon ground turmeric
3 teaspoons chilli powder
1 teaspoon asafoetida powder

Wash the limes and dry thoroughly. Heat 60 ml (2 fl oz/¼ cup) oil in a pan. Add 2 limes and cook over low heat, turning often, for 2 minutes. Remove and repeat until all the limes are done. Do not allow the skin to turn brown. Cool, then cut each lime into eight wedges and cut each wedge into three. Discard the seeds and reserve any juice.

In a dry pan, heat the fenugreek seeds for 1 minute, or until the colour lightens. Take care not to burn the seeds as this will make the pickle bitter. Grind to a fine powder in a mortar and pestle or spice mill.

Heat remaining oil in a heavy-based pan. Add the turmeric, chilli powder, asafoetida and 1 tablespoon salt. Stir quickly and add the limes and reserved juice. Turn off the heat, add the ground fenugreek and stir well.

Spoon immediately into clean, warm jars. Pour a thin layer of warmed oil into each bottle. Seal, label and date. Leave for 1 month before opening to allow the flavours to develop. Store in a cool, dark place for up to 12 months. Refrigerate after opening for up to 6 weeks.

note Dark green limes are too acidic so use pale green/yellow ones. The rind softens with time. Asafoetida powder is a dried plant resin with a very pungent garlicky smell and is available from Indian spice stores.

preparation 20 minutes + cooling * cooking 15 minutes

Fried beef kerala *with Indian lime pickle*

Pickles are very much a part of an Indian meal and, generally, two or three types will be served along with a dish of chilled yoghurt to cool the spiciness of the meal.

INGREDIENTS

oil, for deep-frying, plus 2 tablespoons oil
1 potato, cut into small cubes
500 g (1 lb 2 oz) rump steak, thinly sliced
3 garlic cloves, crushed
1 teaspoon ground black pepper
5 cm (2 inch) piece of ginger, grated with a fine grater into a bowl, placed in a piece of muslin and squeezed to produce 1 tablespoon juice
2 onions, sliced in rings
60 ml (2 fl oz/¼ cup) beef stock
2 tablespoons tomato paste (concentrated purée)
2 teaspoons soy sauce
1 teaspoon chilli powder
60 ml (2 fl oz/¼ cup) lemon juice
3 tomatoes, chopped
80 g (3 oz/½ cup) fresh or frozen peas
Indian lime pickle (recipe on previous page)

Fill a deep, heavy-based saucepan one-third full with oil and heat it to 180°C (350°F), or until a cube of bread browns in 15 seconds. Deep-fry the potato until golden brown. Drain on paper towels.

Put the steak in a bowl and toss with the garlic, pepper and ginger juice. Heat the extra oil and fry the beef quickly in batches over high heat. Keep each batch warm as you remove it. Reduce the heat and fry the onion until golden, then remove.

Cook the beef stock, tomato paste, soy sauce, chilli and lemon juice in the pan over medium heat until reduced. Add the onion, cook for 3 minutes, stir in the tomato and peas, then cook for 1 minute. Add the beef and potato and toss until heated through. Serve with Indian lime pickle.

preparation 15 minutes * cooking 30 minutes * serves 4

Thai sweet chilli sauce

INGREDIENTS

150 g (5 oz) medium–large fresh red chillies
210 g (7½ oz/⅔ cups) sultanas (golden raisins)
3 cloves garlic, chopped
3 cm (1½ inches) finely grated fresh ginger
250 ml (1 cup) white vinegar
410 g (14 oz/1⅔ cups) sugar
155 g (5½ oz/⅔ cup) firmly packed soft brown sugar
1 tablespoon fish sauce

Wearing latex or rubber gloves to protect your hands, cut the chillies in half and remove the seeds.

Combine the chilli, sultanas, garlic, ginger and 60 ml (2 fl oz/¼ cup) of the vinegar in a food processor or blender and process until smooth.

Place the chilli mixture in a large pan, stir in the remaining vinegar, white and brown sugar, fish sauce, ¼ teaspoon salt and 100 ml (3½ fl oz/¼ cup) water. Bring mixture to the boil, stirring until all the sugar has dissolved, then reduce the heat and simmer, stirring often, for 15 minutes, or until the mixture is a slightly thick, syrupy consistency.

Pour immediately into clean, warm jars or bottles and seal. Turn the jars upside down for 2 minutes, then invert and cool. Label and date. Leave for 1 month before opening to allow the flavours to develop. Store in a cool, dark place for up to 12 months. Refrigerate after opening for up to 6 weeks.

note This sauce is quite sweet, yet has a good bite. If you prefer a milder sauce, you can adjust the amount of chilli to your taste. The seeds contain the most heat, so remember to remove these. Wearing gloves helps prevent any irritation to sensitive skin which can sometimes occur when handling chillies.

preparation 30 minutes ✦ cooking 20 minutes

Prawn omelettes *with Thai sweet chilli sauce*

Creamy little omelettes filled with sweet prawn meat and flavoured with coriander and chilli make a simple but special dish. The sauce adds an extra hit of chilli.

INGREDIENTS

500 g (1 lb 2 oz) raw prawns (shrimp)
1½ tablespoons oil
4 eggs, lightly beaten
2 tablespoons fish sauce
8 spring onions (scallions), chopped
6 coriander (cilantro) roots, chopped
2 garlic cloves, chopped
1 small red chilli, seeded and chopped
2 teaspoons lime juice
2 teaspoons grated palm sugar (jaggery) or soft brown sugar
3 tablespoons chopped coriander (cilantro) leaves
1 small red chilli, extra, chopped to garnish
coriander (cilantro) sprigs, to garnish
Thai sweet chilli sauce (recipe on previous page)

Peel the prawns, gently pull out the dark vein from each prawn back, starting from the head end, then chop the prawn meat.

Heat a wok over high heat, add 2 teaspoons of the oil and swirl to coat. Combine the egg with half of the fish sauce. Add 2 tablespoons of the mixture to the wok and swirl to a 16 cm (6 inch) round. Cook for 1 minute, then gently lift out. Repeat with the remaining egg mixture to make 8 omelettes.

Heat the remaining oil in the wok. Add the prawns, spring onion, coriander root, garlic and chilli. Stir-fry for 3–4 minutes, or until the prawns are cooked. Stir in the lime juice, palm sugar, coriander leaves and the remaining fish sauce.

Divide the prawn mixture among the omelettes and fold each into a small firm parcel. Cut a slit in the top and garnish with the chilli and coriander sprigs. Serve with Thai sweet chilli sauce.

preparation 25 minutes * cooking 15 minutes * makes 8

Green tomato pickles

INGREDIENTS
1.25 kg (2 lb 12 oz) green tomatoes
2 onions
120 g (4 ½ oz/½ cup) cooking salt
250 g (9 oz/1 cup) sugar
500 ml (17 fl oz/2 cups) cider vinegar
60 g (2 ¼ oz/½ cup) sultanas (golden raisins)
½ teaspoon mixed spice
½ teaspoon ground cinnamon
2 teaspoons curry powder
pinch cayenne pepper
2 teaspoons cornflour (cornstarch)

Slice tomatoes and onions into thin rounds. Combine with salt in a large non-metallic bowl; add enough water to cover. Place a small plate on top of the vegetables to keep them submerged. Leave overnight.

Drain the tomato and onion and rinse well. Place in a large pan and add the sugar, vinegar, sultanas and spices. Stir over low heat for 5 minutes, or until all the sugar has dissolved. Bring to the boil, then reduce the heat and simmer for 30 minutes, stirring often, or until the vegetables are soft.

Add 2 teaspoons water to the cornflour, mix well and and stir into the mixture. Stir over medium heat until it boils and thickens.

Spoon immediately into clean, warm jars and seal. Turn the jars upside down for 2 minutes, then invert and leave to cool. Label and date. Leave for 1 month before opening to allow the flavours to develop. Store in a cool, dark place for up to 12 months. Refrigerate after opening for up to 6 weeks.

preparation 25 minutes + overnight soaking ✦ cooking 40 minutes

RED OR GREEN?

Green tomatoes are those at the end of the season, which will fail to fully ripen in the cooling weather. Firm, not as juicy as their ripe counterparts and piquant-tasting, green tomatoes make excellent relishes and chutneys. Their suitability for frying is legendary.

Okra pickles

INGREDIENTS

410 ml (14 fl oz/1⅔ cups) cider vinegar
1 teaspoon coriander (cilantro) seeds
1 teaspoon mustard seeds
1 cinnamon stick
4–6 dried small red chillies
2 tablespoons soft brown sugar
1 onion, chopped
500 g (1 lb) small okra, chopped into 1 cm (½ inch) pieces

Place the vinegar, spices, chillies, sugar and 1½ tablespoons water in a large pan and bring to the boil. Reduce the heat and simmer for 5 minutes, then remove from the heat, cover and infuse for 25 minutes.

Strain the vinegar mixture, reserving the chillies, then return to the pan. You will need about 375 ml (13 fl oz/1½ cups) of liquid. Add onion and okra, 2 tablespoons salt and bring to the boil. Reduce heat and simmer over a low heat for 5 minutes, or until the okra is half cooked and there is no more of the sliminess that the okra releases. Skim off any scum during cooking with a skimmer or slotted spoon.

Strain the okra and onion mixture, reserving the liquid, and pack immediately into clean, warm jars, adding two of the reserved chillies to each jar. Fill the jars with the reserved pickling liquid and seal. Turn upside down for 2 minutes, then invert and leave to cool. Label and date. Leave for 1 month before opening to allow the flavours to develop. Store in a cool, dark place for up to 12 months. Refrigerate after opening for up to 6 weeks.

note Use small okra as the larger, older ones tend to be more fibrous. The okra will start to absorb the liquid after 1–2 weeks.

preparation 20 minutes + 25 minutes standing ✶ cooking 10 minutes

Plum sauce

INGREDIENTS

1 large green apple

2 red chillies

1.25 kg (2½ lb) blood plums, halved

460 g (1 lb/2 cups) firmly packed soft brown sugar

375 ml (13 fl oz/1½ cups) white wine vinegar

1 onion, grated

60 ml (2 fl oz/¼ cup) soy sauce

2 tablespoons fresh ginger, finely chopped

2 cloves garlic, crushed

Peel, core and chop the apple and place in a large pan with 125 ml (4 fl oz/½ cup) water. Cover and simmer for 10 minutes, or until the apple is soft. Cut chillies in half lengthways. Remove the seeds and chop finely. Add the plums, sugar, vinegar, onion, soy sauce, ginger, garlic and the chilli.

Bring the mixture to the boil and cook, uncovered, over low–medium heat for 45 minutes. Stir the mixture often throughout the cooking process. Remove sauce from the pan and press it through a coarse strainer set over a large bowl using a wooden spoon. Discard the plum stones. Rinse the pan. Put the sauce back in the clean pan and return to the heat.

Cook the sauce rapidly while stirring until it has thickened slightly—it will thicken even more on cooling.

Pour immediately into clean, warm jars and seal. Turn the jars upside down for 2 minutes, then invert and leave to cool. Label and date. Leave for 1 month before opening to allow the flavours to develop. Store in a cool, dark place for up to 12 months. Refrigerate after opening for up to 6 weeks.

preparation 20 minutes * cooking 1 hour

Spring rolls *with plum sauce*

It is worth making the effort to cook spring rolls from scratch. The wrappers can be purchased from Asian supermarkets. A good plum sauce is an essential accompaniment.

INGREDIENTS

2 dried shiitake mushrooms

250 g (9 oz) minced (ground) pork

1½ tablespoons dark soy sauce

2 teaspoons dry sherry

½ teaspoon Chinese five-spice

2 tablespoons cornflour (cornstarch), plus 1½ teaspoons, extra

80 ml (2½ fl oz/⅓ cup) peanut oil

½ celery stalk, finely chopped

2 spring onions (scallions), thinly sliced

30 g (1 oz) tinned bamboo shoots, finely sliced

40 g (1½ oz/¾ cup) shredded Chinese cabbage

2 garlic cloves, crushed

2 teaspoons finely chopped fresh ginger

¼ teaspoon sugar

¼ teaspoon sesame oil

250 g (9 oz) packet 12 cm (4½ inch) square spring roll wrappers

oil, for deep-frying

plum sauce (recipe on previous page)

Put shiitake mushrooms in a heatproof bowl, cover with boiling water and soak for 20 minutes. Squeeze the mushrooms dry, discard the stems and thinly slice the caps. Mix the pork, soy sauce, sherry, five-spice and 1 tablespoon of the cornflour in a non-metallic bowl and leave for 15 minutes.

Heat 2 tablespoons of the peanut oil in a wok over high heat until nearly smoking, then add the celery, spring onion, bamboo shoots and Chinese cabbage and stir-fry for 3–4 minutes, or until just soft. Season with salt, then transfer to a bowl and set aside. Heat the remaining peanut oil in the wok and cook the garlic and ginger for 30 seconds. Add pork mixture and stir-fry for 2–3 minutes, or until nearly cooked. Combine 1½ teaspoons of the cornflour with 60 ml (2 fl oz/¼ cup) water. Return the cooked vegetables to the wok, then stir in mushrooms. Add sugar, sesame oil and cornflour mixture and stir for 2 minutes. Remove from the heat and cool.

Make a paste with the remaining cornflour and 2–3 teaspoons cold water. Place a spring roll wrapper on a work surface, with one corner pointing towards you. Put 2 teaspoons of the filling in the centre of the wrapper, then brush the edges with a little cornflour paste. Roll up, tucking in the sides as you do so. Repeat with the remaining filling and wrappers. Fill a wok or deep heavy-based saucepan one-third full of oil and heat to 180°C (350°F), or until a cube of bread dropped into the oil browns in 15 seconds. Deep-fry the spring rolls in batches until golden, then drain on crumpled paper towel. Serve hot with the plum sauce.

preparation 45 minutes ✦ cooking 20 minutes ✦ makes 30

Chilli and garlic sauce

INGREDIENTS

8 large dried chillies

4 medium fresh red chillies

4 cloves garlic

125 ml (4 fl oz/½ cup) white vinegar

185 g (6½ oz/¾ cup) sugar

1 tablespoon fish sauce

Remove the stem and seeds from the dried chillies, and break into large pieces. Place in a bowl, cover with boiling water and soak for 15 minutes.

Meanwhile, cut the fresh chillies in half and remove seeds. Wear gloves to protect your hands. Finely chop the garlic. Drain the dried chilli and place in a food processor or blender with the fresh chilli and vinegar and process until smooth.

Pour into a pan and bring to the boil, then reduce the heat, stir in the sugar and garlic, and simmer for 10 minutes, stirring often, until slightly thickened. Add the fish sauce.

Transfer to a heatproof jug and pour immediately into clean, warm jars and seal. Turn the jars upside down for 2 minutes, then invert and cool. Label and date. Leave for 1 month before opening to allow the flavours to develop. Store in a cool, dark place for up to 12 months. Refrigerate after opening.

note THE HEAT IN THE CHILLI DEPENDS ON THE CHILLIES USED AND THEIR SIZE. USUALLY, THE SMALLER THE CHILLI, THE HOTTER IT IS.

preparation 20 minutes + 15 minutes soaking ✦ cooking 15 minutes

Zucchini patties *with chilli and garlic sauce*

Zucchini is an under-valued vegetable that is more versatile than many cooks realise. These delicious patties go well with a pungent chilli and garlic sauce.

INGREDIENTS

300 g (10½ oz) zucchini (courgette), grated
1 small onion, finely chopped
30 g (1 oz/¼ cup) self-raising flour
35 g (1¼ oz/⅓ cup) freshly grated kefalotyri or parmesan cheese
1 tablespoon chopped mint
2 teaspoons chopped flat-leaf (Italian) parsley
pinch freshly grated nutmeg
25 g (1 oz/¼ cup) dry breadcrumbs
1 egg, lightly beaten
olive oil, for pan-frying
lemon wedges, to serve
chilli and garlic sauce (recipe on previous page)

Put the zucchini and onion in the centre of a clean tea towel (dish towel), gather the corners together and twist as tightly as possible to remove all the juices. Combine the zucchini, onion, flour, cheese, mint, parsley, nutmeg, breadcrumbs and egg in a large bowl. Season well, then mix with your hands to form a stiff mixture that clumps together.

Heat the oil in a large frying pan over medium heat. When hot, drop level tablespoons of mixture into the pan and pan-fry for 2–3 minutes, or until well browned all over. Drain well on crumpled paper towels and serve hot, with lemon wedges and the chilli and garlic sauce.

preparation 20 minutes ✦ cooking 15 minutes ✦ makes 16

Red capsicum sauce

INGREDIENTS

2 kg (4 lb 8 oz) red capsicums (peppers)
2 tomatoes
1 large onion, chopped
1 small green apple, peeled, cored and chopped
165 g (5¾ oz/¾ cup) firmly packed soft brown sugar
500 ml (17 fl oz/2 cups) cider vinegar
2 teaspoons black peppercorns
2 tablespoons roughly chopped fresh basil leaves
1 teaspoon cloves
1 bay leaf
3 cloves garlic

Preheat the oven to 200°C (400°F/Gas 6). Roast the capsicums for 35 minutes, or until the skin blisters and blackens. Cut into quarters, remove the skins, seeds and membrane, and chop the flesh.

Score a cross in the base of each tomato. Place in a heatproof bowl and cover with boiling water. Leave for 30 seconds then transfer to cold water and peel the skin away from the cross. Roughly chop the flesh.

Put the capsicum, tomato, onion and apple in a food processor or blender and process until finely chopped. Place in a large pan with the sugar, vinegar and 1 teaspoon salt. Put the peppercorns, basil, cloves, bay leaf and garlic on a square piece of muslin (cheesecloth), tie with string and add to the pan.

Stir over low heat until all the sugar has dissolved. Bring to the boil, then reduce heat and simmer, stirring often, over low–medium heat, for 1 hour 15 minutes, or until the sauce is thick and pulpy. Process in a food processor or blender until smooth.

Pour immediately into clean, warm bottles or jars and seal. Turn upside down for 2 minutes, then invert and leave to cool. Label and date. Leave for 1 month before opening to allow the flavours to develop. Store in a cool, dark place for up to 12 months. Refrigerate after opening.

preparation 30 minutes ✦ cooking 2 hours

Eggplant pickle

INGREDIENTS

800 g (1 lb 12 oz) eggplant (aubergine), cut into 1 cm (½ inch) cubes (2 eggplants)
4 cloves garlic, chopped
50 g (1¾ oz) fresh ginger, chopped
2 red chillies, chopped
125 ml (4 fl oz/½ cup) oil
1 onion, chopped
1 tablespoon ground cumin
1 teaspoon fennel seeds
1 tablespoon ground coriander
½ teaspoon ground turmeric
250 ml (9 fl oz/1 cup) white wine vinegar
160 g (5¾ cup/⅔ cup) sugar

Put the eggplant in a colander set over a bowl and sprinkle with 1 tablespoon salt. Leave for 20 minutes, then rinse well in cold water and pat dry with paper towels. Chop garlic, ginger and chilli in a food processor, adding a teaspoon of water if necessary, to make a paste.

Heat the oil in a large pan, add the onion and cook for 2 minutes, or until soft. Add the garlic paste and the ground cumin, fennel seeds, ground coriander and turmeric, and cook, stirring, for 1 minute. Add the eggplant and cook for 5–10 minutes, or until the eggplant has softened.

Add the white wine vinegar, sugar and 1 teaspoon salt, if necessary, and stir to combine. Cover and simmer gently for 15 minutes, or until soft.

Spoon pickle immediately into clean, warm jars. Use a skewer to remove any air bubbles and seal. Turn the jars upside down for 2 minutes, then invert them and leave to cool. Label and date. Leave for 1 month to allow the flavours to develop. Store jars in a cool, dark place for up to 12 months. Refrigerate after opening for up to 6 weeks.

preparation 20 minutes + 20 minutes standing time ✦ cooking 30 minutes

CHUTNEYS AND RELISHES

Spicy dried fruit chutney

INGREDIENTS

400 g (13 oz) dried apricots
200 g (7 oz) dried peaches
200 g (7 oz) dried pears
250 g (8 oz) raisins
200 g (7 oz) pitted dates
250 g (8 oz) onions
250 g (8 oz) green apples, peeled and cored
4 cloves garlic, finely chopped
1 teaspoon ground cumin
1 teaspoon ground coriander
1 teaspoon ground cloves
1 teaspoon ground cayenne pepper
600 g (1 lb 5 oz/2¾ cups) lightly packed soft brown sugar
600 ml (21 fl oz/2½ cups) malt vinegar

Finely chop the apricots, peaches, pears, raisins, dates, onions and apples. Place in a large pan. Add garlic, cumin, coriander, cloves, cayenne pepper, sugar, vinegar, 2 teaspoons salt and 750 ml (26 fl oz/3 cups) water to the pan.

Stir over low heat until all the sugar has dissolved. Increase the heat and bring to the boil, then reduce heat and simmer, stirring often, over medium heat for 1½ hours, or until the mixture has thickened and the fruit is soft and pulpy. Do not cook over high heat because the liquid will evaporate too quickly and the flavours will not have time to fully develop.

Spoon immediately into clean, warm jars, and seal. Turn upside down for 2 minutes, then invert and leave to cool. Label and date. Leave for 1 month before opening to allow the flavours to develop. Store in a cool, dark place for up to 12 months. Refrigerate after opening.

preparation 20 minutes * cooking 1 hour 35 minutes

THE KING OF FRUITS

There are about 350 varieties of mangoes. Bowen has particularly juicy flesh, its orange skin blushing to red when ripe. Green-skinned mangoes are hard and are a popular ingredient in Southeast Asian salads, pickles and chutneys. Their flesh can be coarsely grated or cut off the stone in thick slices.

Green mango chutney

INGREDIENTS

6 medium (2.6 kg/5 lb 12 oz) firm green mangoes
1 large onion, finely chopped
170 ml (5½ fl oz/⅔ cup) white vinegar
115 g (4 oz/½ cup) firmly packed soft brown sugar
185 g (6½ oz/¾ cup) sugar
2 teaspoons ground ginger
2 teaspoons garam marsala

Remove the peel from the mangoes. Cut the cheeks from the rounded side of each mango and the small amount of flesh around the sides of the seed. Chop flesh into 1 cm (½ inch) pieces and place in a large pan.

Add the remaining ingredients and 1 teaspoon salt to the pan. Stir over medium heat, without boiling, for 5 minutes, or until all the sugar has dissolved.

Bring to the boil, then reduce the heat and simmer for about 45 minutes, or until the mixture is very thick and pulpy. Stir often during cooking to prevent the chutney from sticking and burning on the bottom, especially towards the end of the cooking time.

Spoon immediately into clean, warm jars and seal. Turn the jars upside down for 2 minutes, then invert and leave to cool. Label and date. Leave for 1 month before opening to allow the flavours to develop. Store in a cool, dark place for up to 12 months. Refrigerate after opening for up to 6 weeks.

note This chutney is a traditional accompaniment to Indian-style dishes. Choose firm, green mangoes without bruises or blemishes.

preparation 20 minutes ✦ cooking 50 minutes

Pork vindaloo *with green mango chutney*

Vindaloo is notorious for being hot and spicy. It was invented by the Portuguese in Goa. The tart, fruity chutney is a suitably lively accompaniment.

INGREDIENTS

1 kg (2 lb 4 oz) leg of pork on the bone
6 cardamom pods
1 teaspoon black peppercorns
4 dried chillies
1 teaspoon cloves
10 cm (4 inch) cinnamon stick, roughly broken
1 teaspoon cumin seeds
½ teaspoon ground turmeric
½ teaspoon coriander seeds
¼ teaspoon fenugreek seeds
4 tablespoons clear vinegar
1 tablespoon dark vinegar
4 tablespoons oil
2 onions, finely sliced
10 garlic cloves, finely sliced
5 cm (2 inch) piece of ginger, cut into matchsticks
3 ripe tomatoes, roughly chopped
4 green chillies, chopped
1 teaspoon jaggery or soft brown sugar
green mango chutney (recipe on previous page)

Trim away any excess fat from the pork, remove the bone and cut the pork into 2.5 cm (1 inch) cubes. Reserve the bone.

Split open the cardamom pods and remove the seeds. Finely grind the cardamom seeds, peppercorns, dried chillies, cloves, cinnamon stick, cumin seeds, turmeric, coriander seeds and fenugreek seeds in a spice grinder or pestle and mortar.

In a large bowl, mix ground spices with the vinegars. Add pork and mix thoroughly to coat well. Cover and marinate in the fridge for 3 hours.

Heat the oil in a karhai or casserole over low heat and fry the onion until lightly browned. Add the garlic, ginger, tomato and chilli and stir well. Add the pork, increase the heat to high and fry for 3–5 minutes, or until browned. Add 250 ml (1 cup) water and any of the marinade liquid left in the bowl, reduce the heat and bring slowly back to the boil. Add the jaggery and the pork bone. Cover tightly and simmer for about 1½ hours, stirring occasionally until the meat is very tender. Discard the bone. Season with salt, to taste. Serve with pickle on the side.

preparation 20 minutes + 3 hours marinating ∗ cooking 1 hour 50 minutes ∗ serves 4

Chow chow

INGREDIENTS

650 g (1 lb 7 oz) cauliflower, cut into small florets

1 Lebanese (short) cucumber, peeled, seeded and cut into 2 cm (¾ inch) cubes

375 g (12 oz) green beans, trimmed and cut into 3 cm (1¼ inch) lengths

1 red and 1 green capsicum (pepper), cut into cubes

1 litre (4 cups) cider vinegar

230 g (8 oz/1 cup) firmly packed soft brown sugar

2 tablespoons mustard powder

2 tablespoons yellow mustard seeds

2 teaspoons ground turmeric

pinch cayenne pepper

60 g (2¼ oz/½ cup) plain (all-purpose) flour

420 g (14 oz) can red kidney beans, rinsed and drained

310 g (10 oz/1½ cups) can corn kernels, drained

Blanch the cauliflower florets, cucumber, beans and capsicum separately in boiling water. Drain and cool quickly under cold running water. Set aside.

Reserve 250 ml (9 fl oz/1 cup) of the vinegar. Combine the remaining vinegar with the sugar, mustard powder and seeds, turmeric and cayenne pepper in a large pan. Stir over low heat to dissolve the sugar.

Whisk the reserved vinegar and the flour together in a bowl. Add to the pan and whisk over medium heat for 5 minutes, or until the mixture boils and thickens. Add the blanched vegetables, kidney beans and corn kernels. Mix thoroughly, bring to the boil, and cook, stirring often, for another 5 minutes.

Spoon immediately into clean, warm jars and seal. Turn upside down for 2 minutes, then invert and leave to cool. Label and date. Leave for 1 month before opening to allow the flavours to develop. Store in a cool, dark place for up to 12 months. Refrigerate after opening for up to 6 weeks.

preparation 30 minutes * cooking 20 minutes

Nectarine and lemongrass chutney

INGREDIENTS

3 large green chillies
3 stalks lemongrass, white part only
1.5 kg (3 lb 5 oz) nectarines, stones removed, roughly chopped
3 cloves garlic, finely chopped
2 tablespoons grated fresh ginger
1 large onion, chopped
2 teaspoons ground coriander
500 ml (17 fl oz/2 cups) white wine vinegar
280 g (10 oz/1½ cups) lightly packed soft brown sugar

Cut the chillies in half, remove the seeds from two and finely slice all the chillies. Bruise the lemongrass with the back of a knife and slice finely.

Place all the ingredients in a large pan and add 1 teaspoon salt. Stir over low heat for 5 minutes, or until all the sugar has dissolved.

Bring to the boil, then reduce the heat and simmer for 45–50 minutes, or until chutney is thick and pulpy. Stir often to prevent the chutney from sticking or burning on the bottom.

Spoon immediately into clean, warm jars and seal. Turn jars upside down for 2 minutes, then invert and leave to cool. Label and date. Leave for 1 month before opening to allow the flavours to develop. Store in a cool, dark place for up to 12 months. Refrigerate after opening for up to 6 weeks.

note IT IS BEST TO WEAR GLOVES WHEN HANDLING CHILLIES TO PROTECT YOUR FINGERS FROM THE HEAT OF THE SEEDS AND FLESH.

preparation 25 minutes * cooking 1 hour

Chilli and red capsicum relish

INGREDIENTS

4 large red capsicums (peppers)
2 large onions, roughly chopped
1 red chilli
2 cloves garlic
500 ml (17 fl oz/2 cups) white vinegar
1.5 kg (3 lb 5 oz/6½ cups) sugar, approximately

Quarter the capsicums and remove the seeds and white membrane. Roughly chop the flesh and place in a food processor or blender with the onion, chilli, garlic and some salt. You may need to do this in batches. Process until smooth and place in a large pan.

Add vinegar, bring to the boil and boil for 10–15 minutes, or until tender. Measure the capsicum mixture and measure an equal amount of sugar. Add the sugar, stirring until all the sugar has dissolved, and then slowly bring to the boil. Brush down the sides of the pan with a wet brush to remove any undissolved sugar crystals. Remove any scum during cooking with a skimmer or slotted spoon.

Boil for 15 minutes, stirring often, then reduce the heat and simmer for 30 minutes, or until the relish is thick and pulpy.

Spoon immediately into clean, warm jars and seal. Turn the jars upside down for 2 minutes, then invert and cool. Label and date. Leave for 1 month before opening to allow the flavours to develop. Store in a cool, dark place for up to 12 months. Refrigerate after opening for up to 6 weeks.

note BRUSHING THE SIDES OF THE PAN DISSOLVES ANY SUGAR CRYSTALS WHICH, IF LEFT, COULD CAUSE THE RELISH TO CRYSTALLIZE WHEN CHILLED.

preparation 15 minutes * cooking 1 hour

Banana, tamarind and date chutney

INGREDIENTS

125 g (4 oz) tamarind pulp
90 g (3¼ oz/ ¼ cup) caster (superfine) sugar
1 teaspoon ground cumin
½ teaspoon cayenne pepper
2 tablespoons grated fresh ginger
250 g (8 oz/1½ cups) pitted dates, chopped
60 g (2¼ oz/ ½ cup) slivered almonds
8 firm ripe bananas, chopped

Put the tamarind pulp in a bowl with 750 ml (26 fl oz/3 cups) boiling water. Cool, then break up with a fork. Pour into a sieve placed over a bowl and press out the liquid. Discard the seeds.

Put the liquid in a large pan with the sugar, cumin, cayenne pepper and 1 teaspoon salt. Stir over low heat until all the sugar has dissolved.

Add the ginger, dates and almonds. Bring to the boil, then reduce the heat and simmer for 10 minutes. Add the banana and cook, stirring often, for 30 minutes, or until soft and pulpy.

Spoon chutney immediately into clean, warm jars. Use a metal skewer to remove any air bubbles and seal. Turn upside down for 2 minutes, then invert and leave to cool. Label and date. Leave for 1 month before opening to allow the flavours to develop. Store in a cool, dark place for up to 12 months. Refrigerate after opening for up to 6 weeks.

note TAMARIND PULP IS AVAILABLE IN MOST ASIAN GROCERY STORES.

preparation 25 minutes * cooking 45 minutes

Banana Tamarind & Date Chutney

Blueberry relish

INGREDIENTS

1 kg (2 lb 4 oz/6½ cups) blueberries
500 g (1 lb 2 oz/2 cups) sugar
185 ml (6 fl oz/¾ cup) white wine vinegar
1 teaspoon cayenne pepper
½ teaspoon ground allspice (pimento)
¼ teaspoon ground cinnamon
60 ml (2 fl oz/¼ cup) lemon juice (reserve any pips and rind)

Place the blueberries in a large pan with the sugar, vinegar, cayenne pepper, allspice, cinnamon, lemon juice, 1 teaspoon salt and 125 ml (4 fl oz/½ cup) water. Roughly chop the rind of half a lemon and, with the pips, place on a square of muslin (cheesecloth) and tie securely with string. Add to the pan. Stir over low heat for 5 minutes, or until all the sugar has dissolved.

Bring to the boil, then reduce the heat and simmer, stirring often, for 50–55 minutes, or until the relish is thick and syrupy.

Spoon immediately into clean, warm jars and seal. Turn the jars upside down for 2 minutes, then invert and leave to cool. Label and date. Leave for 1 month before opening to allow the flavours to develop. Store in a cool, dark place for up to 12 months. Refrigerate after opening for up to 6 weeks.

note BLUEBERRIES ARE VERY DELICATE FRUIT, SO BE CAREFUL NOT TO OVERCOOK THEM OR THEY WILL BREAK UP AND FALL APART.

preparation 15 minutes ✦ cooking 1 hour

Roast peach chutney

INGREDIENTS

2 kg (4 lb 8 oz) ripe slipstone peaches
2 onions, thinly sliced
2 cloves garlic, crushed
375 g (13 oz/1½ cups) sugar
600 ml (2 fl oz/2½ cups) cider vinegar
1 tablespoon yellow mustard seeds
2 cinnamon sticks
1 teaspoon ground ginger

Preheat the oven to 210°C (415°F/Gas 6–7). Score a cross in the base of each peach. Place peaches in a heatproof bowl and cover with boiling water. Leave for 30 seconds, then cover with cold water and peel the skin away from the cross. Cut the peaches in half and remove the stone.

Line 2–3 rectangular pans with baking paper. Place the peaches in a single layer on the paper and roast for 30 minutes, or until they start to brown on the edges. (A lot of juice will come out of the peaches.) Tip the peaches and any juices into a large pan, and add the onion, garlic, sugar, vinegar, mustard seeds, cinnamon sticks and ginger. Stir over heat until all the sugar has dissolved.

Return to the boil, then reduce the heat and simmer for 1¼–1½ hours, or until chutney is thick and pulpy. Stir occasionally to break up the peaches and prevent the mixture from sticking to the bottom of the pan. Remove the cinnamon sticks.

Spoon immediately into clean, warm jars and seal. Turn upside down for 2 minutes, then invert and leave to cool. Label and date. Leave for 1 month before opening to allow the flavours to develop. Store in a cool, dark place for up to 12 months. Refrigerate after opening for up to 6 weeks.

preparation 30 minutes ✦ cooking 2 hours

Red capsicum relish

INGREDIENTS

1 kg (2 lb 4 oz) red capsicums (peppers)
375 ml (13 fl oz/1½ cups) red wine vinegar
2 teaspoons black mustard seeds
2 red onions, thinly sliced
4 cloves garlic, chopped
1 teaspoon grated fresh ginger
2 apples, peeled, cored and grated
1 teaspoon black peppercorns
230 g (8 oz/1 cup) firmly packed soft brown sugar

Remove the seeds and membranes and thinly slice the capsicums. Put in a large pan with the vinegar, mustard seeds, onion, garlic, ginger and apple. Place the peppercorns on a square of muslin (cheesecloth), tie securely with string, and add to the pan. Simmer for 30 minutes, or until the capsicum is soft.

Add the sugar and stir over low heat, without boiling, until all the sugar has dissolved. Bring to the boil, stirring often, then reduce the heat and simmer, for 1¼ hours, or until relish is thick and pulpy. Discard the muslin bag.

Spoon immediately into clean, warm jars and seal. Turn jars upside down for 2 minutes, then invert; cool. Label and date. Leave for 1 month before opening to allow the flavours to develop. Store in a cool, dark place for up to 12 months. Refrigerate after opening for up to 6 weeks.

preparation 40 minutes ✦ cooking 1 hour 50 minutes

FRESH IS BEST

Many people only know beetroot from tins, but taking the trouble to prepare it in its fresh state is well worth the work. Buy bulbs that are about the same size, avoiding any very large ones that can be woody. And, only buy specimens with fresh-looking leaves and stems attached.

Beetroot relish

INGREDIENTS

750 g (1 lb 10 oz/5⅓ cups) fresh beetroot, peeled and coarsely grated
1 onion, chopped
400 g (13 oz) green apples, peeled, cored and chopped
410 ml (14 fl oz/1⅔ cups) white wine vinegar
95 g (3¼ oz/½ cup) lightly packed soft brown sugar
125 g (4½ oz/½ cup) sugar
2 tablespoons lemon juice

Place all the ingredients and 2 teaspoons salt in a large pan and stir over low heat, without boiling, until all the sugar has dissolved. Bring to the boil and boil, stirring often, for 20–30 minutes, or until the beetroot and onion are tender and the relish is reduced and thickened.

Spoon immediately into clean, warm jars, and seal. Turn upside down for 2 minutes, then invert and leave to cool. Label and date. Leave for 1 month before opening to allow the flavours to develop. Store in a cool, dark place for up to 12 months. Refrigerate after opening for up to 6 weeks.

preparation 25 minutes ✦ cooking 35 minutes

Spicy pumpkin chutney

INGREDIENTS

1 kg (2 lb 1 oz/6½ cups) pumpkin, peeled and cut into small chunks
2 tablespoons oil
2 teaspoons cumin seeds
½ teaspoon ground cinnamon
½ teaspoon ground coriander
1 onion, chopped
2 cloves garlic, crushed
60 g (2¼ oz/½ cup) sultanas
80 g (2¾ oz/⅓ cup) firmly packed soft brown sugar
125 ml (4 fl oz/½ cup) malt vinegar
185 ml (6 fl oz/¾ cup) orange juice
1 tablespoon chopped fresh coriander (cilantro) leaves

Preheat the oven to 200°C (400°F/Gas 6). Place the pumpkin in a baking dish and drizzle with the oil. Bake for 40 minutes.

Put the pumpkin and the remaining ingredients, except the coriander leaves, in a large pan. Add ½ teaspoon salt and bring mixture to the boil. Reduce heat and simmer for 10–15 minutes, stirring often, or until the mixture thickens.

Gently stir in the coriander and remove from the heat. Spoon immediately into clean, warm jars and seal. Turn upside down for 2 minutes, then invert and leave to cool. Label and date. Leave for 1 month before opening to allow the flavours to develop. Store in a cool, dark place for up to 12 months. Refrigerate after opening for up to 6 weeks.

note To get a thick and chunky mixture, use harder pumpkin varieties that take longer to cook, such as Queensland Blue or Jarrahdale.

preparation 20 minutes ✦ cooking 55 minutes

Pineapple chutney

INGREDIENTS

1 kg (2 lb 4 oz) ripe pineapple
2 onions, chopped
½ teaspoon ground ginger
½ teaspoon ground cloves
1 teaspoon ground cinnamon
165 g (5¾ oz/¾ cup) firmly packed soft brown sugar
125 ml (4 fl oz/½ cup) white wine vinegar
60 g (½ cup) raisins

Peel the pineapple and remove the tough eyes. Cut into quarters, remove and discard the hard centre core and dice the flesh. Combine with the onion, ginger, cloves, cinnamon, sugar, vinegar and raisins in a large pan and stir over low heat until all the sugar has dissolved.

Bring the mixture to the boil, then reduce the heat and simmer for 1½ hours, stirring often, until the mixture has reduced and thickened and the pineapple is soft.

Spoon immediately into clean, warm jars, and seal. Turn the jars upside down for 2 minutes, then invert and leave to cool. Label and date. Leave for 1 month before opening to allow flavours to develop. Store in a cool, dark place for up to 12 months. Refrigerate after opening for up to 6 weeks.

note THE PINEAPPLE IS RIPE IF IT HAS A FRAGRANT PINEAPPLE AROMA AND THE CENTRAL LEAF PULLS OUT EASILY.

preparation 30 minutes * cooking 1 hour 35 minutes

Autumn chutney

INGREDIENTS

500 g (1 lb) firm pears, peeled, cored and chopped
500 g (1 lb) green apples, peeled, cored and chopped
500 g (1 lb) tomatoes, peeled and chopped
500 g (1 lb) onions, chopped
5 celery sticks, sliced
3 cloves garlic, thinly sliced
2 teaspoons grated fresh ginger
350 g (11 oz/3¾ cups) sultanas (golden raisins)
1 litre (4 cups) white vinegar
2 teaspoons ground cinnamon
2 teaspoons ground ginger
460 g (1 lb/2 cups) lightly packed soft brown sugar

Combine all the ingredients, except the sugar, in a large pan. Bring to the boil, then reduce the heat and simmer for 45 minutes.

Add sugar and stir until all the sugar has dissolved. Bring to the boil and cook for 30–35 minutes, stirring often, or until the chutney has reduced and thickened.

Spoon chutney immediately into clean, warm jars and seal. Turn upside down for 2 minutes, then invert and leave to cool. Label and date. Leave for 1 month before opening to allow the flavours to fully develop. Store in a cool, dark place for up to 12 months. Refrigerate after opening.

preparation 25 minutes * cooking 1 hour 25 minutes

Piccalilli

INGREDIENTS
400 g (13 oz) cauliflower, cut into florets
1 small cucumber, chopped
200 g (6½ oz) green beans, cut into 2 cm (¾ inch) lengths
1 onion, chopped
2 carrots, chopped
2 celery sticks, chopped
100 g (3½ oz/⅓ cup) salt
250 g (9 oz/1 cup) sugar
1 tablespoon mustard powder
2 teaspoons ground turmeric
1 teaspoon ground ginger
1 fresh red chilli, seeded and finely chopped
1 litre (4 cups) white vinegar
200 g (7 oz) frozen broad beans, thawed, peeled
60 g (2¼ oz/½ cup) plain (all-purpose) flour

Combine the cauliflower, cucumber, beans, onion, carrot, celery and salt in a large bowl. Add enough water to cover the vegetables, and top with a small upturned plate to keep the vegetables submerged. Leave to soak overnight.

Drain the vegetables well and rinse under cold running water. Drain the vegetables again. Combine the vegetable mixture with the sugar, mustard, turmeric, ginger, chilli and all but 185 ml (6 fl oz/¾ cup) of the vinegar in a large pan. Bring to the boil, then reduce the heat and simmer for 3 minutes. Stir in the broad beans. Remove any scum from the surface with a skimmer or slotted spoon.

Blend the flour with the remaining vinegar and stir it into the vegetable mixture. Stir until the mixture boils and thickens. Spoon immediately into clean, warm jars and seal. Turn the jars upside down for 2 minutes, then invert. Label and date. Leave for 1 month before opening to allow the flavours to develop. Store in a cool, dark place for up to 12 months. Refrigerate after opening for up to 6 weeks.

preparation 30 minutes + overnight soaking * cooking 10 minutes

Roasted tomato relish

INGREDIENTS

2 kg (4 lb 8 oz) tomatoes, halved
2 onions (310 g/10 oz), chopped
2 small red chillies, seeded and chopped
1 teaspoon paprika or Hungarian smoked paprika
350 ml (12 fl oz/1⅓ cups) white wine vinegar
340 g (12 oz/1⅓ cups) sugar
60 ml (2 fl oz/¼ cup) lemon juice
1 teaspoon grated lemon rind

Preheat the oven to 150°C (300°F/Gas 2). Line a baking tray with foil and then baking paper. Place the tomato halves cut-side-up on the baking tray and cook for 1 hour. Sprinkle with the onion and cook for another hour.

Cool slightly, then remove the tomato skins and roughly chop the flesh. Place the tomato, onion, chilli, paprika, vinegar, sugar, lemon juice, lemon rind and 2 teaspoons salt into a large pan and stir until all the sugar has dissolved.

Bring to the boil, then reduce the heat and simmer for 45 minutes, or until the relish is thick and pulpy. Stir often to prevent the relish from burning or sticking.

Spoon immediately into clean, warm jars and seal. Turn the jars upside down for 2 minutes, then invert and leave to cool. Label and date. Leave for 1 month before opening to allow the flavours to develop. Store in a cool, dark place for up to 12 months. Refrigerate after opening for up to 6 weeks.

note IF AVAILABLE, HUNGARIAN SMOKED PAPRIKA GIVES THIS RELISH A LOVELY SMOKY FLAVOUR. IT IS AVAILABLE AT SPECIALITY SPICE SHOPS AND DELICATESSENS.

preparation 20 minutes ✦ cooking 2 hours 50 minutes

Cheese-filled crepes *with tomato relish*

The unfilled crepes can be made up to three days in advance but must be refrigerated with baking paper to separate them. Sharp and creamy cheeses go well with the relish.

INGREDIENTS

CREPES

165 g (5¾ oz/1⅓ cups) plain (all-purpose) flour

500 ml (17 fl oz/2 cups) milk

3 eggs, lightly beaten

30 g (1 oz) butter, melted

CHEESE FILLING

400 g (14 oz) ricotta cheese, crumbled

100 g (3½ oz/⅔ cup) grated mozzarella cheese

25 g (1 oz/¼ cup) freshly grated parmesan cheese

pinch freshly grated nutmeg

3 tablespoons chopped flat-leaf (Italian) parsley

roasted tomato relish (recipe on previous page)

25 g (1 oz/¼ cup) freshly grated parmesan cheese

2 tablespoons extra virgin olive oil, to drizzle

To make the crepes, sift the flour and ½ teaspoon salt into a bowl. Make a well in the centre and add the milk gradually, stirring constantly until the mixture is smooth. Add the eggs, little by little, beating well until smooth. Cover and set aside for 30 minutes.

Heat a crepe pan or non-stick frying pan and brush lightly with the melted butter. Pour 60 ml (2 fl oz/¼ cup) of batter into the pan, swirling quickly to thinly cover the base. Cook for 1 minute, or until underside is golden. Turn and cook the other side until golden. Transfer to a plate and continue with the remaining batter, stacking the crepes as you go.

Preheat the oven to 200°C (400°F/Gas 6) and lightly grease a shallow ovenproof dish with butter or oil.

To make the filling, mix all the ingredients together and season well.

To assemble, spread 1 heaped tablespoon of filling over each crepe, leaving a 1 cm (½ inch) border. Fold the crepe in half and then in quarters. Place in the ovenproof dish, so that they overlap but are not crowded. Spoon the tomato sauce over the crepes, sprinkle with parmesan and drizzle with the extra virgin olive oil. Bake for 20 minutes, or until heated.

preparation 25 minutes ✦ cooking 1 hour 10 minutes ✦ makes about 12

Traditional chilli jam

INGREDIENTS

8 large dried red chillies
2 whole heads of garlic
300 g (10 oz) red Asian or French shallots
250 ml (9 fl oz/1 cup) peanut oil
100 g (3½ oz) small dried shrimps
1 teaspoon shrimp paste
120 g (4 oz) palm sugar, grated
3 tablespoons tamarind concentrate
2 teaspoons finely grated lime rind

Remove the stems and seeds from the chillies and break into large pieces. Place in a bowl, cover with hot water and soak for 15 minutes. Divide the garlic into cloves. Peel and thinly slice the garlic and shallots. Drain the chilli and pat dry.

Heat half the oil in a wok over a medium–low heat and gently fry the garlic, shallots and chilli, stirring often, until golden brown. Remove and drain on paper towels.

Place the shrimp in a spice mill, food processor or mortar and pestle and process or pound until fine. Add the shrimp paste and fried garlic, shallots and chilli, and process to a smooth paste.

Reheat wok and add the remaining oil and the paste mixture. Cook for 5 minutes, stirring, or until it is very aromatic. Stir in the palm sugar, tamarind, lime rind, 1 teaspoon salt and 100 ml (3½ fl oz) water. Bring to the boil, stirring constantly, for 5–8 minutes, or until mixture has thickened. Take care not to burn the bottom of the pan. Spoon immediately into clean, warm jars and seal. Store chilli jam in a cool, dark place for 6–12 months. Refrigerate after opening for up to 6 weeks.

note This jam is thick and paste-like and will firm on cooling. Ingredients such as dried shrimps, shrimp paste, palm sugar and tamarind concentrate are available from Asian food stores.

preparation 20 minutes + 15 minutes soaking* cooking 20 minutes

Dried apricot chutney

INGREDIENTS

500 g (1 lb 2 oz) dried apricots
1 large onion, chopped
3 cloves garlic, finely chopped
2 tablespoons grated fresh ginger
500 ml (17 fl oz/2 cups) cider vinegar
230 g (8 oz/1 cup) firmly packed soft brown sugar
125 g (4½ oz/1 cup) sultanas
2 teaspoons mustard seeds, crushed (see Note)
2 teaspoons coriander seeds, crushed
½ teaspoon ground cumin
80 ml (2½ oz/⅓ cup) orange juice
½ teaspoon grated orange rind

Put the apricots in a bowl, cover with 2 litres (8 cups) water and leave to soak for 2 hours. Drain and put 1 litre (4 cups) of the soaking water into a large pan. Make up the amount with fresh water if there is not enough. Chop the apricots. Put the apricots and all the ingredients, except the orange juice and rind, into the pan. Add 1 teaspoon salt.

Stir the mixture over low heat for 5 minutes, or until all the sugar has dissolved. Bring to the boil, cover and boil for 45 minutes, or until thick and pulpy. Stir often, especially towards the end of the cooking time so the mixture does not stick and burn. Remove any scum during cooking with a skimmer or slotted spoon.

Stir in the orange juice and rind. Spoon immediately into clean, warm jars. Use a skewer to remove any air bubbles, then seal. Turn upside down for 2 minutes, then invert and leave to cool. Label and date. Leave for 1 month to allow the flavours to develop. Store in a cool, dark place for up to 12 months. Refrigerate after opening for up to 6 weeks.

note CRUSHING THE MUSTARD AND CORIANDER SEEDS HELPS TO RELEASE THEIR AROMA. YOU CAN USE THE BACK OF A LARGE, HEAVY KNIFE TO CRUSH THE SEEDS, OR A MORTAR AND PESTLE, OR PUT THEM IN A THICK PLASTIC BAG AND CRUSH THEM WITH A ROLLING PIN.

preparation 20 minutes + 2 hours soaking* cooking 50 minutes

Sweet corn relish

INGREDIENTS

1 green capsicum (pepper), seeded and finely chopped
1 red capsicum (pepper), seeded and finely chopped
3 x 420 g (14 oz) cans corn kernels, drained
1 tablespoon yellow mustard seeds, crushed (see Note)
2 teaspoons celery seeds, crushed
1 large onion, finely chopped
600 ml (21 fl oz/2½ cups) white wine or cider vinegar
2 tablespoons mustard powder
230 g (8 oz/1 cup) firmly packed soft brown sugar
1 teaspoon ground turmeric
2 tablespoons cornflour (cornstarch)

Place all the ingredients, except the cornflour, in a large pan. Add 1 teaspoon salt and stir over low heat for 5 minutes, or until all the sugar has dissolved. Simmer for 50 minutes, stirring frequently.

Combine the cornflour with 2 tablespoons water. Add to the pan and cook, stirring, for 2–3 minutes, or until the mixture boils and thickens.

Spoon immediately into clean, warm jars. Use a skewer to remove air bubbles and seal. Turn jars upside down for 2 minutes, then invert and leave to cool. Label and date. Leave for 1 month before opening to allow the flavours to develop. Store in a cool, dark place for up to 12 months. Refrigerate after opening.

note CRUSH THE MUSTARD AND CELERY SEEDS IN A MORTAR AND PESTLE, OR PLACE IN A PLASTIC BAG AND CRUSH WITH A ROLLING PIN, TO RELEASE THE AROMA.

preparation 15 minutes * cooking 1 hour

Apple, date and pecan chutney

INGREDIENTS

2 brown onions, chopped
1.2 kg (2 lb 11 oz) green apples, peeled, cored and chopped into small chunks
400 g (13 oz/2½ cups) dates, seeded and chopped
125 g (4 oz/1 cup) pecans, chopped
2 teaspoons cumin seeds
2 teaspoons finely chopped fresh ginger
315 ml (10¾ oz/1¼ cups) white vinegar
125 g (4½ oz/½ cup) sugar

Put onion and 125 ml (4 fl oz/½ cup) water in a large pan. Bring to the boil, then reduce heat and simmer, covered, for 10–15 minutes, or until onion is soft. Add the apple, and simmer, covered, for 15–20 minutes, or until the apple has softened. Stir often.

Add the dates, pecans, cumin seeds, ginger, vinegar, sugar, ½ teaspoon salt and 60 ml (2 fl oz/¼ cup) water. Stir over low heat for 5 minutes, or until all the sugar has dissolved. Simmer for 5 minutes, or until thick.

Spoon immediately into clean, warm jars. Use a skewer to remove any air bubbles, then seal. Turn upside down for 2 minutes, then invert and leave to cool. Label and date. Leave for 1 month before opening to allow the flavours to develop. Store in a cool, dark place for up to 12 months. Refrigerate after opening for up to 6 weeks. Serve with roast pork, ham, cold meats and cheese.

preparation 20 minutes * cooking 45 minutes

Sweet tomato and eggplant chutney

INGREDIENTS

2 kg (4 lb 8 oz) ripe tomatoes
500 g (1 lb 2 oz) brown onions, chopped
500 g (1 lb 2 oz) slender eggplant (aubergine), finely chopped
4 cloves garlic, finely chopped
2 teaspoons sweet paprika
2 teaspoons brown mustard seeds, crushed
500 g (1 lb 2 oz/2 cups) sugar
600 ml (21 fl oz/2½ cups) white vinegar

Score a cross in the base of each tomato and place 4–5 at a time in a heatproof bowl and cover with boiling water. Leave for 30 seconds then transfer to cold water and peel the skin away from the cross. Roughly chop the flesh and place in a large pan.

Add the remaining ingredients to the pan. Add 2 teaspoons salt and stir over low heat for 5 minutes, or until all the sugar has dissolved. Bring to the boil, then reduce heat and simmer, for 50–60 minutes, or until the chutney is thick and pulpy. Stir often. Remove any scum during cooking with a skimmer or slotted spoon. Do not cook the mixture over high heat or the liquid will evaporate too quickly and the flavours won't have sufficient time to develop.

Transfer to a heatproof jug and immediately pour into clean, warm jars and seal. Turn jars upside down for 2 minutes, then invert and leave to cool. Label and date. Leave for 1 month before opening to allow flavours to develop. Store in a cool, dark place for up to 12 months. Refrigerate after opening for up to 6 weeks. Serve with cold meats, steak, chicken or fish.

note To achieve the richest flavour, it is best to choose very ripe tomatoes for this recipe.

preparation 20 minutes ✱ cooking 1 hour 10 minutes

Mostarda di fruta

INGREDIENTS

175 g (6 oz) glacé fruit
1 teaspoon cornflour (cornstarch)
315 ml (10½ fl oz/1¼ cups) white wine
1 tablespoon honey
3 cloves
1 tablespoon yellow mustard seeds
¼ teaspoon ground nutmeg
½ teaspoon grated fresh ginger
2 cinnamon sticks, broken into pieces
1 tablespoon lemon juice

Using a pair of scissors, chop the fruit into even-sized pieces. Mix the cornflour with 1 teaspoon water and blend to a paste.

Place 200 ml (6½ fl oz) water in a pan with the wine, honey, cloves, mustard seeds, nutmeg, ginger and cinnamon sticks. Bring to the boil, add cornflour mixture. Simmer for 5 minutes, or until mixture thickens.

Add the glacé fruit and lemon juice, and simmer for 10–15 minutes, or until the fruit is soft and the mixture is thick. Spoon immediately into clean, warm jars and seal. Turn upside down for 2 minutes, then invert and leave to cool. Label and date. Store for a week before eating.

note MOSTARDA DI FRUTA IS POPULAR IN ITALIAN CUISINE. IT IS SERVED WITH COLD MEATS, POULTRY AND GAME, AND HAS A VERY SWEET FLAVOUR.

preparation 10 minutes * cooking 20 minutes

Tomato and chilli relish

INGREDIENTS

1 kg (2 lb) tomatoes
3 cooking apples (500 g/1 lb), peeled, cored and grated
2 onions, chopped
1 teaspoon grated fresh ginger
4 cloves garlic, chopped
1–2 long red chillies, sliced
230 g (1 cup) firmly packed soft brown sugar
250 ml (1 cup) cider vinegar

Cut a cross at the base of each tomato, place in a large bowl, cover with boiling water and leave for 30 seconds, or until the skins start to spilt. Transfer to a bowl of cold water. Peel away the skin, roughly chop the tomatoes and place in a large pan.

Add the remaining ingredients to the pan and stir over low heat until all the sugar has dissolved. Bring to the boil, then reduce the heat and simmer, stirring often, for 2–2¼ hours, or until the relish has reduced and thickened.

Spoon immediately into clean, warm jars, and seal. Turn the jars upside down for 2 minutes, then invert and leave to cool. Label and date. Leave for 1 month before opening to allow the flavours to develop. Store in a cool, dark place for up to 12 months. Refrigerate after opening for up to 6 weeks.

preparation 20 minutes * cooking 2 hours 20 minutes

Dried fruits

Dried fruits make a simple, yet delicious, snack to nibble on instead of crisps or lollies. You can also use crisp dried fruits, lightly dusted with icing sugar, (confectioners' sugar) as a garnish on a fruit mousse. Most fruits can be dried, except berries and those with a high water content. It is important to keep dried fruits cool and dry, otherwise they will discolour or go mouldy. They can be kept in an airtight container in a cool, dry place for up to 2 weeks.

Before you start the drying process, think about how you are going to slice the fruit to make it look its best. Apples, for example, are best sliced across the middle, while pears are best sliced lengthways. Fruit such as rhubarb can be shaped during the cooling process.

A mandolin is a hand-held slicer with extremely sharp, adjustable blades. Always use the safety shield when slicing. If you have one, a mandolin will make slicing some of the smaller fruit much easier. If you don't have a mandolin, you just need a good, sharp knife, so be careful! You can pick the fruit you wish to dry because of its shape, for example, star fruit. Adding lemon juice helps the fruit keep its colour, as does the sugar, but check your fruit regularly while it is drying to make sure it doesn't burn or get too brown. Cool any fruit thoroughly before storing it in an airtight container—it should keep for a few days before softening but can be quickly refreshed in the oven until it dries out again.

PINEAPPLE

Peel and remove the tough eyes from a medium-sized pineapple, then cut the flesh into 2 mm (⅛ inch) slices. Pat the slices dry with paper towels and spread them out on baking trays lined with baking paper. Sprinkle the pineapple slices lightly with sugar and cook in an oven at the lowest possible temperature for 3 hours. Turn the slices over approximately halfway through the cooking process. Check every now and then to make sure the pineapple pieces don't get too dark or burn. Remove the pineapple carefully from the baking trays when dry and cool completely before storing in an airtight container.

APPLES AND PEARS

Slice 2 apples and 2 pears as thinly as you can, about 2 mm (⅛ inch) thick, if possible, leaving the skin and core intact. Cut the apples through the middle to get a pretty star-shaped pattern from the core. Cut the pears through their length. Put both the apple and pear slices in a bowl, sprinkle them with a little lemon juice and toss to coat thoroughly. Pat the fruit slices dry with paper towels and spread out on baking trays lined with baking paper. Sprinkle the apple and pear slices lightly with sugar and cook in an oven at the lowest possible temperature for 2½–3 hours. Turn the slices over approximately halfway through the cooking process. Check now and then to make sure fruit pieces don't get too dark or burn. Remove apple and pear slices carefully from the tray when dry. Cool completely before storing in an airtight container.

STAR FRUIT

Cut 2 or 3 star fruit into 2 mm (⅛ inch) slices and sprinkle with the juice of half a lemon. Pat the star fruit slices dry with paper towels and spread out on baking trays lined with baking paper. Sprinkle lightly with sugar and cook in an oven at the lowest possible temperature for 2–2½ hours. Turn the slices over approximately halfway through the cooking process. Check every now and then to make sure they don't get too dark or burn. Remove the star fruit carefully from the tray when dry and cool completely before storing in an airtight container.

RHUBARB

Remove the string and trim the ends from 2 or 3 rhubarb stems and slice into long, thin strips along the length of the fruit. Pat rhubarb slices dry with paper towels and spread out on baking trays lined with baking paper. Sprinkle lightly with sugar. Cook in an oven at the lowest possible temperature for 2½ –3 hours. Turn the slices over approximately halfway through the cooking process. Check every now and then to make sure the rhubarb pieces don't get too dark or burn. Remove the rhubarb carefully from the tray when dry and then cool completely before storing in an airtight container. If you want to be a little more creative, you can try wrapping the cooked rhubarb around the handle of a wooden spoon when cooling.

note To keep the fruit as crisp as possible, spread a thin layer of uncooked rice on the base of an airtight container, cover with baking paper and top with the fruit. The rice will absorb any excess moisture. Drying times may vary greatly, depending on the fruit chosen, the season and oven temperatures. Once opened, refrigerate for 1–2 weeks.

Curds

Fruit curds are delicious spread on toast, scones, croissants or pikelets. They can also be used as fillings for sponge cakes, crêpes, tarts or meringues. When placed in decorated jars, they always make popular gifts. Or, pour into small jars, label, date and sell at your next school fête. The mixture of fruit and butter gives a rich, creamy consistency and taste which is hard to resist. They will keep for up to two months in the refrigerator, should they not get eaten well before then.

LEMON CURD

Combine 1½ tablespoons finely grated lemon rind, 185 g (6 oz/¾ cup) soft unsalted butter, 185 ml (6 fl oz/¾ cup) lemon juice and 250 g (9 oz/1 cup) caster (superfine) sugar in a heatproof bowl. Place the bowl over a pan of gently simmering water, without touching the water, and stir the mixture until the butter has melted and all the sugar has dissolved. Add 12 egg yolks and stir constantly until the mixture thickens and coats the back of a spoon. This will take about 15–20 minutes—the heat must remain low or the mixture will curdle. Strain the mixture, reheat and then pour into clean, warm jars. Seal while hot, label and date. Keep in the refrigerator for up to 2 months. Makes about 600 ml (2½ cups)

MANGO AND LIME CURD

Cut cheeks from 2 large mangoes, cutting on either side of stone, peel and chop the flesh. Blend flesh in a food processor or blender until smooth. Push through a fine sieve. You will need 315 ml (11 fl oz/1¼ cups) of strained mango purée. Combine the purée with ½ teaspoon finely grated lime rind, 80 ml (2½ fl oz/⅓ cup) strained lime juice, 160 g (5½ oz/⅔ cup) soft unsalted butter, 250 g (9 oz/1 cup) sugar and 4 beaten eggs in a heatproof bowl. Place bowl over a pan of simmering water, without touching the water. Stir constantly until the butter has melted and the sugar has dissolved. Stir for 15–20 minutes, or until the mixture thickens and coats the back of a spoon. Remove from the heat, pour into clean, warm jars and seal while hot. Keep in refrigerator for up to 2 months. Makes about 875 ml (3½ cups)

PASSIONFRUIT CURD

Beat 4 eggs and strain them into a heat-proof bowl. Stir in 185 g (6½ fl oz/¾ cup) caster (superfine) sugar, 80 ml (2½ fl oz/⅓ cup) lemon juice, 200 g (7 oz/¾ cup) soft butter, 125 g (4½ fl oz/½ cup) passionfruit pulp and 3 teaspoons grated lemon rind. Place bowl over a pan of simmering water, without letting it touch the water, and stir until butter has melted and the sugar has dissolved. Stir constantly for 15–20 minutes, or until mixture thickly coats the back of a spoon. Spoon into clean, warm jars. Seal while hot. Refrigerate when cool. Keep in the refrigerator for up to 2 months. Makes 600 ml (2½ cups)

VANILLA BEAN AND LEMON CURD

Place 2 teaspoons grated lemon rind, 125 ml (4 fl oz/½ cup) lemon juice, 125 g (4½ oz/½ cup) soft unsalted butter and 185 g (6½ fl oz/ ¾ cup) vanilla-infused caster (superfine) sugar (see Note) in a pan. Stir over low heat until all the sugar has dissolved. Lightly beat 4 egg yolks and slowly drizzle into the lemon mixture while stirring. Return the mixture to the heat and cook over low heat, stirring constantly, for about 5 minutes, or until thickened. Pour into clean, warm jars and seal while hot. Keep in the refrigerator for up to 2 months. Makes 375 ml (1½ cups)

note To make vanilla sugar, store a whole vanilla bean with the caster sugar in an airtight container for at least 1 week prior to use. Remove the vanilla bean before use. If washed and dried thoroughly, and stored in an airtight container, the vanilla bean can be reused three or four times.

STRAWBERRY CURD

Hull 250 g (9 oz) strawberries, chop roughly and put in pan with 185 g (6½ fl oz/¾ cup) caster (superfine) sugar, 125 g (4 oz/½ cup) soft unsalted butter, 1 tablespoon lemon juice and 1 teaspoon grated lemon rind. Stir over a low heat until butter has melted and the sugar dissolved. Simmer gently for 5 minutes, then remove from heat. Lightly beat 4 egg yolks in a large bowl, then slowly drizzle them into the strawberry mixture while stirring. The mixture will thicken as you add it. Return to low heat and then cook for 2 minutes while stirring. Do not allow the mixture to boil or the curd will separate. Pour into clean, warm jars and seal while hot. Keep in the refrigerator for up to 2 months. Makes 500 ml (2 cups)

DRIED APRICOT CURD

Place 100 g (3½ oz/⅔ cup) finely chopped dried apricots in a bowl, cover with 125 ml (4 fl oz/½ cup) boiling water, and stand for 30 minutes. Stir to form a lumpy paste. Beat 4 eggs well and strain into a heatproof bowl, stir in 125 ml (4 fl oz/½ cup) lemon juice, 125 g (4½ fl oz/½ cup) caster (superfine) sugar, 180 g (6 oz/¾ cup) soft unsalted butter and the apricot paste. Place bowl over a pan of simmering water, without touching the water. Stir until the butter has melted and sugar dissolved. Stir constantly for about 15–20 minutes, or until mixture thickly coats the back of a spoon. Spoon into clean, warm jars and seal while hot. Keep in the refrigerator for up to 2 months.Makes 2½ cups (600 ml/20 fl oz)

Microwave jams

These recipes are based on an 850 watt microwave. If your microwave wattage is different, cooking times may vary. Take extra care when cooking jams in a microwave, due to the extreme heat.

APRICOT JAM

Put two small plates in the freezer. Halve and remove the stones from 500 g (1 lb 2 oz) fresh apricots and roughly chop. Place in a microwave-proof bowl with 2 tablespoons lemon juice. Place the white pith from 1 lemon on a square of muslin (cheesecloth), tie securely with string and place in bowl. Cook, uncovered, on high for 6 minutes, stirring once or twice. Cool slightly, then measure. Add 250 g (9 oz/1 cup) sugar for every cup of fruit mixture and stir until all the sugar has dissolved. Cook, uncovered, on high for 15–20 minutes, or until the mixture reaches setting point. Test for setting point a couple of times during cooking (see page 8). If ready, discard the bag. Carefully pour the very hot (85°C/185°F) jam into clean, warm jars. Turn jars upside down for 2 minutes, then invert and leave to cool. Label and date. Makes 500 ml (2 cups)

STRAWBERRY JAM

Put two small plates in the freezer . Hull and quarter 750 g (1 lb 10 oz) fresh strawberries and place in a microwave-proof bowl with 60 ml (2 fl oz/⅓ cup) lemon juice. Place the white pith from 1 lemon on a square of muslin (cheesecloth), tie securely with string and place in bowl. Cook, uncovered, on high for 6 minutes, or until mixture is soft and pulpy, stirring once or twice. Cool slightly then measure. Add 250 g (9 oz/1 cup) sugar for every cup of fruit mixture and stir until sugar has dissolved. Cook, uncovered, on high for 15–20 minutes, or until mixture reaches setting point. Test for setting point during cooking (see page 8). When jam is ready, discard bag. Carefully pour the very hot (85°C/185°F) jam into clean, warm jars and seal. Turn the jars upside down for 2 minutes, then invert and leave to cool. Label and date. Makes 500 ml (2 cups)

DRIED FIG JAM

Put two small plates in freezer. Remove stalks from 500 g (1 lb 2 oz) dried figs and place in a microwave-proof bowl with 375 ml (13 fl oz/1½ cups) water and 2 tablespoons lemon juice. Place the white pith from 1 lemon on a square of muslin (cheesecloth), tie securely with string and place in bowl. Cook, uncovered, on high for 10 minutes, or until mixture is soft and pulpy, stirring once or twice. Cool slightly then measure. Add 250 g (9 oz/1 cup) sugar for every cup of fruit mixture and stir until all the sugar has dissolved. Cook, uncovered, on high for 15–20 minutes, or until mixture reaches setting point. Test for setting point a couple of times during cooking (see page 12). Discard the bag. Carefully pour the very hot (85°C/185°F) jam into clean, warm jars. Turn jars upside down for 2 minutes, then invert and leave to cool. Label and date. Makes 1 litre (4 cups)

CITRUS MARMALADE

Put two small plates in the freezer. Remove the rind from a grapefruit, a lemon and an orange. Remove the pith and roughly chop the flesh. Remove the seeds. Place pith and seeds onto a square of muslin (cheesecloth) and tie securely with string. Place the rind and the bag in a microwave-proof bowl and cover with 375 ml (13 fl oz/1½ cups) water. Cook, uncovered, on high for 10 minutes, or until rind is soft. Cool slightly, then measure. Add 250 g (9 oz/1 cup) sugar for every cup of the fruit mixture and stir until dissolved. Cook, uncovered, on high for 20–25 minutes, or until mixture reaches setting point. Test for setting point a couple of times during cooking (see page 8). Discard bag. Carefully pour the very hot (85°C/185°F) jam into clean, warm jars. Turn the jars upside down for 2 minutes, then invert and leave to cool. Label and date. Makes 500 ml (2 cups)

MIXED BERRY JAM

Put two small plates in the freezer. Place 500 g (1 lb 2 oz) mixed berries in a microwave-proof bowl with 60 ml (2 fl oz/¼ cup) lemon juice. Place the white pith from 1 lemon onto a square of muslin (cheesecloth), tie securely with string and place in bowl. Cook, uncovered, on high for 6 minutes or until the mixture is soft and pulpy, stirring once or twice. Cool slightly then measure. Add 250 g (9 oz/1 cup) sugar for every cup of fruit mixture and stir until all the sugar has dissolved. Cook, uncovered, on high for 15–20 minutes, or until the mixture reaches setting point. Test for setting point a couple of times during cooking (see page 8). If ready, discard the bag. Carefully pour the very hot (85°C/185°F) jam into clean, warm jars. Turn jars upside down for 2 minutes, then invert and leave to cool. Label and date. Makes 500 ml (2 cups)

RASPBERRY JAM

Put two small plates in freezer. Place 500 g (1 lb 2 oz) raspberries in a microwave-proof bowl with 60 ml (2 fl oz/¼ cup) lemon juice. Place the white pith from 1 lemon onto a square of muslin (cheesecloth), tie securely with string and place in bowl. Cook, uncovered, on high for 6 minutes, or until mixture is soft and pulpy, stirring once or twice. Cool slightly and measure. Add 250 g (9 oz/1 cup) sugar for every cup of fruit mixture and stir until all the sugar has dissolved. Cook, uncovered, on high for 15–20 minutes, or until the mixture reaches setting point. Test for setting point a couple of times during cooking (see page 8). Discard the bag. Carefully pour the very hot (85°C/ 185°F) jam into clean, warm jars. Turn the jars upside down for 2 minutes, then invert and leave to cool. Label and date. Makes 500 ml (2 cups)

Liqueur fruits

Served over ice cream, with ricotta cheese or mascarpone, with brioche or panettone, or over toasted waffles or crêpes, these luscious, decadent liqueur fruits make an ideal finale to any meal. Make sure the fruit you use is just ripe and free of blemishes. Liqueur fruits should be left for a month before using to allow flavours to develop and must be refrigerated after opening.

APRICOTS IN RUM

Place 185 g (6½ oz/¾ cup) sugar in a pan with 500 ml (17 fl oz/2 cups) water. Stir over low heat until sugar has dissolved. Bring to the boil, add 500 g (1 lb 2 oz) dried apricots, reduce heat and simmer for 3 minutes. Remove pan from the heat and stir in 185 ml (6 fl oz/¾ cup) dark rum. Make sure temperature is at least 85°C (185°F) and spoon into a clean, warm 1 litre (4 cup) jar. Seal while hot and leave to cool. Label and date. Leave for 1 month before using. Store in a cool, dry place for 6 months. Makes 1 litre (4 cups)

note IT IS VERY IMPORTANT TO USE A GOOD-QUALITY RUM FOR THIS RECIPE AS IT WILL DRASTICALLY AFFECT THE FLAVOUR.

PRUNES IN PORT

Place 125 ml (4 fl oz/½ cup) water, 90 g (3¼ oz/⅓ cup) sugar and 8 cloves into a large pan. Stir over low heat until the sugar has dissolved. Bring to the boil, then reduce heat and simmer for 15 minutes. Add 600 g (1 lb 5 oz) pitted prunes, thinly sliced rind of 1 orange and about 500 ml (17 fl oz/2 cups) port. Make sure the temperature is at least 85°C (185°F) and spoon into a 1 litre (4 cup) clean, warm jar. Seal while hot and leave to cool. Label and date. Leave for 1 month before using. Store in a cool, dry place for 6 months. Makes 1 litre (4 cups) Note: The prunes will swell during standing.

MUSCAT FRUITS

Place 150 g (5½ oz) prunes, 150 g (5½ oz) small dried figs, stems removed, 100 g (3½ oz) dried sliced apples, 100 g (3½ oz) dried peach halves, 100 g (3½ oz) dried apricot halves, 100 g (3½ oz) raisins, 2 strips orange rind, 2 cinnamon sticks, halved, 4 whole cloves and 750 ml (26 floz/3 cups) clear apple juice in a large non-metallic bowl. Cover and soak overnight. Place in a large pan and bring to the boil, then reduce the heat and simmer for 5 minutes. Remove the pan from the heat and stir in 250 ml (9 fl oz/1 cup) liqueur muscat. Make sure the temperature is at least 85°C (185°F) and spoon fruit mixture and syrup into clean, warm, wide-neck jars. Seal, label and date. Leave for 1 month before using. Store in a cool, dark place for 6 months. Makes about 1.125 litres (4½ cups)

PRESERVED FIGS IN BRANDY

Place 750 g (1 lb 10 oz/3 cups) sugar in a pan along with 375 ml (13 fl oz/1½ cups) water. Stir over low heat until all the sugar has dissolved. Bring to the boil, then reduce heat, add 400 g (14 oz) firm fresh figs and simmer for 5 minutes, or until the figs begin to soften (this will depend on ripeness of the figs). Lift figs from the syrup with a slotted spoon, allowing as much syrup as possible to drain off and place them in clean, warm, wide-neck jars. Repeat with remaining figs. Gently shake jars to help settle the figs. Some syrup will accumulate in jars, so place the slotted spoon over the mouth of the jars and tip the excess syrup back into the pan. Bring syrup to the boil and boil for 10 minutes, or until it thickens. Remove from heat, allow any bubbles to subside and pour 375 ml (13 fl oz/1½ cups) into a large heatproof jug, reserving any remaining syrup. Stir in 375 ml (13 fl oz/1½ cups) brandy and pour into jars to cover the figs. If there is not enough brandy syrup to cover, combine small quantities of the reserved syrup and some of the brandy in a jug and cover figs. Make sure temperature is at least 85°C (185°F) and seal while hot. Label and store for 1 month before using. Store in a cool, dry place for 6 months. Refrigerate after opening. Makes 1 litre (4 cups)

PEACHES IN BRANDY

Place 6–8 (1 kg/2 lb 4 oz) firm ripe slipstone peaches in a large bowl, cover with boiling water and leave for 30 seconds. Remove peaches using a slotted spoon and refresh in a bowl of icy water. Remove skins, cut the peaches in half and gently twist and pull apart to remove stones. Place 250 ml (9 fl oz/1 cup) water and 125 g (4½ oz/½ cup) sugar in a large pan, and stir over low heat until all sugar has dissolved. Bring to the boil, add peach halves and simmer for 2–3 minutes. Remove the peaches with a slotted spoon and place into a 1 litre (4 cup) clean, warm jar. Add a split vanilla bean to the syrup and simmer for 5 minutes. Stir in 250 ml (9 fl oz/1 cup) brandy, then, making sure the temperature is at least 85°C (185°F), pour the syrup over the peaches, placing the vanilla bean inside the jar. Ensure that the fruit is fully covered with the syrup, leaving a very small space at the top of the jar. Seal and label. Leave for 2 weeks before using. Store in a cool, dry place for up to 6 months. Makes 1 litre (4 cups)

Fruit pastes

Fruit pastes are a delicious method for preserving an overabundance of fruit. They may take a while to cook, but they keep for well for up to a year because of their high concentration of sugar. They are delicious served with coffee, as part of a cheeseboard or with cold meats.

TO PACKAGE AND STORE THE PASTES:
Spread into the prepared tin and smooth with a palette knife. Cut the pastes into small squares, diamonds or triangles with a hot knife. Place a blanched or slivered almond in the centre of each piece or roll in caster sugar to coat, if desired. Wrap in foil and store in an airtight container in a cool, dry place. Disposable foil tins are ideal for storing fruit pastes. Spread the hot fruit mixture into them and press a piece of greaseproof paper onto the mixture before wrapping.

note AS THE MIXTURE THICKENS, IT WILL START TO SPLATTER. MAKE SURE YOU USE A LARGE, DEEP-SIDED PAN AND WRAP A TEA TOWEL (DISH TOWEL) AROUND YOUR HAND WHILE STIRRING.

QUINCE PASTE
Line a 28 x 18 cm (11 x 7 inch) tin with baking paper. Peel and core 2 kg (4 lb 8 oz) quinces, reserving cores. Cut into chunks and place in a large pan. Chop the cores, place on a square of muslin (cheesecloth), tie securely with string and add to pan along with 500 ml (17 fl oz/2 cups) water and 2 tablespoons lemon juice. Cook, covered, over low heat for 30–40 minutes, or until soft and tender. Cool slightly, squeeze any juices from bag and discard it. Purée fruit in a blender or food processor until smooth, then press through a fine sieve. Weigh purée and return it to the pan. Gradually add an equivalent measure of sugar (1 kg/ 2 lb 4 oz fruit purée = 1 kg/2 lb 4 oz sugar). Stir over low heat, without boiling, until sugar has dissolved. Cook, stirring with a wooden spoon to prevent from sticking and burning, for 45–60 minutes, or until the mixture leaves side of pan and is difficult to push the wooden spoon through.

APRICOT PASTE
Line a 28 x 18 cm (11 x 7 inch) tin with baking paper. Select 2 kg (4 lb 8 oz) apricots (you will need some to be a little green to help gel the paste). Remove stalks, stones and any blemishes. Cut the apricots into quarters and the remainder in half. Place in a large pan with 250 ml (9 fl oz/1 cup) water and 2 tablespoons lemon juice. Bring to the boil, then reduce the heat and simmer, covered, for 15–20 minutes, or until fruit is soft and tender. Cool slightly. Purée the fruit in a blender or food processor until smooth, then press through a fine sieve. Weigh the purée and return it to the pan. Gradually add an equivalent measure of sugar (1 kg/2 lb 4 oz fruit purée = 1 kg/2 lb 4 oz sugar). Stir over low heat, without boiling, until all sugar has dissolved. Cook, stirring with a wooden spoon to prevent sticking and burning, for 45–60 minutes, or until

mixture leaves the side of the pan and it is difficult to push the wooden spoon through. (If the mixture starts to stick to the bottom of the pan, transfer it to a heatproof bowl, clean the pan and return the mixture to the clean pan to continue cooking.)

PLUM PASTE

Line a 28 x 18 cm (11 x 7 inch) tin with baking paper. Select 1.5 kg (3 lb) plums (you will need some to be a little green to help gel the paste). Remove the stalks, stones and any blemishes, then cut into quarters. Place in a large pan with 250 ml (9 fl oz/1 cup) water and 2 tablespoons lemon juice. Bring to the boil, then reduce the heat and simmer, covered,for 20–30 minutes, or until fruit is soft and tender. Cool slightly. Purée the fruit in a blender or food processor until smooth, then press through a fine sieve. Weigh the purée and return it to the pan. Gradually add an equal measure of sugar (1 kg/2 lb 4 oz fruit purée = 1 kg/2 lb 4 oz sugar). Stir constantly over low heat, without boiling, until all the sugar has dissolved. Cook, stirring with a wooden spoon to prevent from sticking and burning, for 45–60 minutes, or until mixture leaves the side of pan and is hard to push the wooden spoon through. (If the mixture starts to stick to the bottom of the pan, transfer it to a heatproof bowl, clean the pan and return the mixture to the clean pan to continue the cooking.)

PEACH PASTE

Line a 28 x 18 cm (11 x 7 inch) tin with baking paper. Remove the stalks, blemishes and stones from 2 kg (4 lb 8 oz) peaches (you will need some to be a little green to help gel the paste). Cut each peach into 8 pieces and place in a large pan with 250 ml (9 fl oz/1 cup) water and 3 tablespoons lemon juice. Bring to the boil, reduce heat and simmer, covered, for 20–30 minutes, or until fruit is soft and tender. Cool slightly. Pureé fruit in a blender or food processor until it is smooth, then press through a fine sieve. Weigh the purée and return it to the pan. Gradually add an equal measure of the sugar (1 kg/2 lb 4 oz fruit purée = 1 kg/2 lb 4 oz sugar) to the pan. Stir constantly over low heat, without boiling, until all sugar has dissolved. Cook, stirring with a wooden spoon to prevent from sticking and burning, for 45–60 minutes, or until the mixture leaves the side of the pan and it is difficult to push the wooden spoon through. (If the mixture starts to stick to the bottom of pan, transfer it to a heatproof bowl, clean the pan and return the mixture to the clean pan to continue cooking.)

Heat processing

Make the most of the abundance of fruit available each season and preserve them to be enjoyed for up to a year later. They will only keep for up to a week in the refrigerator, once opened.

Use either bottling jars with glass lids, spring clips and rubber seals, or Kilner bottles with metal lids and rubber seals. Ensure the bottles fit snugly into the pot and will be fully submerged in the simmering water.

TEN STEPS TO HEAT PROCESSING

1. Choose just ripe or slightly underripe fruit, without blemishes.
2. Thoroughly wash and dry the bottles.
3. Pack the fruit tightly to allow for shrinkage during processing.
4. Dip the rubber seals into boiling water to sterilize them before placing them on the bottles.
5. To make the sugar syrup, place the sugar and water in a pan. Stir over low heat until dissolved. Brush the sides of the pan with a wet pastry brush to remove any undissolved sugar. Bring to the boil, and boil for 3 minutes.
6. Cover the fruit with hot syrup (85°C/185°F). Tap the bottles while filling to remove any air bubbles.
7. Carefully close the lids.
8. Put a folded tea towel on the base of the stockpot. Fill the pot with warm water (38°C) to submerge the bottles.
9. Gradually bring the water to simmering (88–90°C), this may take 25–30 minutes, then simmer steadily for the processing time. Do not allow the water to boil. Check the water level regularly and top up with boiling water, if required.
10. When processing is complete, remove pot from the heat and remove some water. Wear rubber gloves or use tongs to remove the bottles. Do not put any pressure on lids. Place on a wooden board and cool overnight. Label and date.

To test that the seals on the spring-clip bottles are secure, release the clip and, with your fingertips, grip the rim of the lid and carefully lift the bottles. The seals will hold their own weight if properly processed. If they do not, store in the refrigerator and consume within 2 days.

PEARS
Mix 1 litre (4 cups) water with 1 teaspoon salt and 1 tablespoon lemon juice, or ½ teaspoon citric acid, in a large bowl. Peel 2.75 kg (5 lb 10 oz) beurre bosc pears, halve and remove cores. Place each pear in the lemon water mixture. Make a sugar syrup by dissolving 750 g (1 lb 10 oz/3 cups) sugar in 1.5 litres (6 cups) boiling water and 1½ teaspoons citric acid or 60 ml (2 fl oz/¼ cup) lemon juice. Arrange fruit in six 500 ml (17 fl oz/2 cup) bottles. Follow the 10 steps to heat processing. Cook for 30 minutes.

APRICOTS AND PLUMS
Score a cross in the base of 2.5 kg (5 lb 8 oz) apricots or 2.5 kg (5 lb 8 oz) plums. Place in a heatproof bowl and cover with boiling water. Leave for 30 seconds, then transfer to cold water. Peel away skins, halve and remove stones. Make a sugar syrup by dissolving 500 g (1 lb 2 oz/2 cups) sugar in 1 litre (4 cups) boiling water. Arrange fruit in six 500 ml (17 fl oz/2 cup) bottles. Follow the 10 steps to heat processing. Cook for 15 minutes.

PEACHES
Score a cross in the base of 2.5 kg (5 lb 8 oz) slipstone peaches. Place in a heatproof bowl and cover with boiling water. Leave for 30 seconds, then transfer to cold water. Remove skins, halve and remove stones. Cut into 1.5 cm (½ inch) slices. Make a sugar syrup by dissolving 375 g (13 oz/1½ cups) sugar in 1.25 litres (2 lb 8 oz/4½ cups) boiling water. Arrange the fruit in six 500 ml (17 fl oz/2 cup) bottles. Follow the 10 steps to heat processing. Cook for 15 minutes.

TOMATOES
Score a cross in the base of 2.5 kg (5 lb 8 oz) Roma tomatoes. Place in a heatproof bowl and cover with boiling water. Leave for 30 seconds, then transfer tomatoes to cold water and peel away skin. Make a brine of 4½ teaspoons salt , 1 tablespoon citric acid and 1.5 litres (6 cups) water. Stir to dissolve over low heat for 2–3 minutes. Arrange tomatoes in six 500 ml (17 fl oz/2 cup) bottles. Follow then 10 steps to heat processing, using the brine instead of sugar syrup. Cook for 20 minutes.

Index

Published in 2012 by Murdoch Books Pty Limited.

Murdoch Books Australia
Pier 8/9
23 Hickson Road
Millers Point NSW 2000
Phone: +61 (0) 2 8220 2000
Fax: +61 (0) 2 8220 2558
www.murdochbooks.com.au
info@murdochbooks.com.au

Murdoch Books UK Limited
Erico House, 6th Floor
93–99 Upper Richmond Road
Putney, London SW15 2TG
Phone: +44 (0) 20 8785 5995
Fax: +44 (0) 20 8785 5985
www.murdochbooks.co.uk
info@murdochbooks.co.uk

For Corporate Orders & Custom Publishing contact Noel Hammond,
National Business Development Manager, Murdoch Books Australia.

Publisher: Anneka Manning
Production: Karen Small

A cataloguing-in-publication entry is available from the catalogue of the National Library of Australia at www.nla.gov.au.
A catalogue record for this book is available from the British Library.

Printed by 1010 Printing International Limited, China.

IMPORTANT: Those who might be at risk from the effects of salmonella poisoning (the elderly, pregnant women, young children and those suffering from immune deficiency diseases) should consult their doctor with any concerns about eating raw eggs.

OVEN GUIDE: You may find cooking times vary depending on the oven you are using. For fan-forced ovens, as a general rule, set the oven temperature to 20°C (35°F) lower than indicated in the recipe.

We have used 20 ml (4 teaspoon) tablespoon measures. If you are using a 15 ml (3 teaspoon) tablespoon add an extra teaspoon of the ingredient for each tablespoon specified.